"Sue Roffey has written an essential book for educators across th ciples encompass foundational pillars for the promotion of lear children and youth. This is a user-friendly volume with many pra and educational administrators around the world will benefit greatly from th these pages. I highly recommend it to educators, parents, psychologists, counsellors, and anyone interested in flourishing and the creation of a just and vibrant society."

Isaac Prilleltensky, *Professor, PhD, University of Miami*

"As Sue Roffey articulates so intelligently, passionately and clearly, wellbeing is both complex and contextual. This book provides a comprehensive and clear framework for considering how best to grow contextual wellbeing across your whole school using her well established ASPIRE principles. A fabulous foundation for whole-school development, and a much-needed voice for wellbeing equity."

Helen Street, *Founder of Contextual Wellbeing and Positive Schools,*
Honorary Fellow, The University of Western Australia

"This excellent book shows how to enable pupils to flourish in school now and how we can help all to thrive in future. The ASPIRE principles build social justice. I highly recommend it."

Anthony Seldon, *Co-chair of the Times Education*
Commission Report: Bringing out the Best

"Wellbeing is not merely a means to an end. It is the end goal we all aspire to, and how ultimately, we measure the success of our lives. Dr Sue Roffey's ASPIRE books provide a pathway for schools to build wellbeing for all - students, educators, and community. Dr Roffey illustrates how the ASPIRE principles can underpin the values of a school, inform and drive policy, practice and structure, and guide teacher-student relationships. This work is pro-active, comprehensive and universal and aims at nothing less than a revitalisation of education."

Denise Quinlan, *Director of the New Zealand Institute of Wellbeing and Resilience*

"I have no hesitation in recommending this book to all educators - wellbeing and learning must be a focus for us all if we are to build successful schools and more importantly successful families of the future. Sue's ASPIRE framework provides us with a clear structure to frame our thinking."

Maureen McKenna, *Former Executive Director of Education, City of Glasgow*

"For true educational change we need to know to what we aspire. Drawing from both her rich experience and the best educational science, Roffey points us toward educational contexts in which students want to learn. She points us beyond a narrow focus on cognitive achievement, to the kind of schools where human development, intellectual, social, and emotional, is the goal. Beyond piecemeal reform she describes cultures of education where both students and teachers can flourish. This is a book that can truly lead the way of positive school change."

Richard M. Ryan, *Professor, Institute for Positive Psychology and Education,*
Australian Catholic University, North Sydney and Distinguished Professor,
College of Education, Ewha Womans University, South Korea

"There has been some talk post pandemic of doing things differently in schools and not just returning to default settings in search of a more rewarding and compelling school vision for educators and students. This (Sue's) inspiring and thoughtful book provides the narrative for this work. It poses the question, does the education system as we know it meet the needs of learners and educators or is there another way? A way which provides the skills that employers want, the happiness that parents seek for their children and a way of teaching and learning which helps to retain and recruit those who work in our schools. Joining the conversation and planning for a better future for our schools starts with Sue's book which covers key aspects of what an education system fit for the 21ˢᵗ century must include."

Andy Mellor, *National Wellbeing Director for Schools Advisory Service, National Association of Head Teachers National President 18/19, Strategic Lead for Carnegie centre of excellence for mental health in schools.*

"Sue's aspirations and vision for a truly inclusive, critical, and hopeful approach to education is one that is sorely needed. Sue's work guides schools, educators, and psychologists to see wellbeing as something to be actively pursued and cultivated, rather than just the absence of mental ill-health. The realisation of the ASPIRE principles would mark a systems change in how we 'do' education."

Dan O'Hare, *Educational Psychologist, Senior Lecturer, University of Bristol and founder of edpsy.org.uk*

"As educators and educational leaders, we continually seek pathways to profoundly impact generations of learners. Dr Roffey's work is a vital contribution to this journey, offering both inspiration and practical strategies for creating educational environments where every child can flourish. This book presents a transformative vision for education, deeply resonating with the Global Citizenship Foundation's mandate to transform education for human and planetary flourishing. I hope this essential resource reaches practitioners and policymakers committed to nurturing inclusive, sustainable, and equitable environments where every child can realize their full potential and flourish."

Aaryan Salman, *Director-General, Global Citizenship Foundation, India*

"As we enter a more and more tumultuous century, we and our children will have to master social/political and climate challenges as well as disinformation. Sue Roffey, in her passionately argued and practical book shows us the way. Based on her vast experience in positive education, she describes how children, educators and larger society may achieve greater wellbeing and resilience through a shared learning environment. In her ASPIRE program, she elaborates the basic elements for transforming today's education systems, and indeed our lives, into one that allows the development of thriving children. An important read!"

Marten W. de Vries, *Emeritus Professor, Social Psychiatry and Public Mental Health, Maastricht University, Netherlands; Chair, Mind Venture International Institute; Knighted in the Order of the Dutch Lion*

"Sue Roffey is a force of nature and this book is everything you would expect: intelligent, insightful and driven by a burning sense of social justice. The question of what education is too often overlooked. The consequences are clear: the wellbeing of educators, as well as children and young people, is not in good shape. Research-informed, humane and practical, the ASPIRE model is the antidote we so badly need. Despite the name, this is not aspirational stuff. It is urgent reading that should rocket to the top of every educator's reading pile. Grab it with both hands and implement it in your schools. Your colleagues, pupils and their families will thank you for it for many years to come."

James Mannion, *Director, Rethinking Education and Co-author, 'Fear is the Mind Killer'*

ASPIRE to Wellbeing and Learning for All in Early Years and Primary

This truly accessible resource shows primary school practitioners how to help every student feel valued and included in school so that they develop confidence, resilience, love of learning, a positive sense of self and healthy relationships.

Sue Roffey presents a visionary and unique approach to education underpinned by clear principles that can be practically applied in all settings. It is aligned with healthy child development, and addresses what all children need if they are to learn and thrive, including those who experience difficulties and disadvantages. She envisages an education system fit for purpose where all pupils can thrive and make progress in learning, where wellbeing for everyone is at the heart of every school. She uses ASPIRE as an acronym for Agency, Safety, Positivity, Inclusion, Respect and Equity. These principles, when threaded through everything that happens in a school, can genuinely enhance both wellbeing and learning. This resource features a chapter for each principle which explores *what* this means, *why* it matters and *how* it can be applied in early years, primary classrooms and across primary schools. Although visionary, the book is based on both substantial evidence and good practice, with each chapter supported by case studies from across the world.

The book demonstrates the positive difference each principle makes to children in primary school settings as well as teachers, parents and the overall community. It is a must-read for primary school teachers, tutors, school leaders, psychologists, parents and anyone who wants an education system that is inclusive, holistic and effective for all students.

Sue Roffey is a teacher, psychologist, academic, author, speaker and social activist. She is also Honorary Associate Professor at University College London, UK, and Director of Growing Great Schools Worldwide. She has previously published *Creating the World We Want to Live In* (Routledge, 2021), *The Primary Behaviour Cookbook* (Routledge, 2018) and *The Secondary Behaviour Cookbook* (Routledge, 2018).

ASPIRE to Wellbeing and Learning for All in Early Years and Primary

The Principles Underpinning Positive Education

Sue Roffey

Routledge
Taylor & Francis Group

LONDON AND NEW YORK

First published 2024
by Routledge
4 Park Square, Milton Park, Abingdon, Oxon OX14 4RN

and by Routledge
605 Third Avenue, New York, NY 10158

Routledge is an imprint of the Taylor & Francis Group, an informa business

British Library Cataloguing-in-Publication Data
A catalogue record for this book is available from the British Library

Library of Congress Cataloging-in-Publication Data
Names: Roffey, Sue, author.
Title: ASPIRE to wellbeing and learning for in all in primary and early years : the principles underpinning positive education / Sue Roffey.
Description: Abingdon, Oxon ; New York, NY : Routledge, 2024. | Includes bibliographical references and index. | Identifiers: LCCN 2023056892 (print) | LCCN 2023056893 (ebook) | ISBN 9781032549507 (hardback) | ISBN 9781032549484 (paperback) | ISBN 9781003428237 (ebook)
Subjects: LCSH: Education, Primary--Aims and objectives. | Educational equalization.
Classification: LCC LB1507 .R64 2024 (print) | LCC LB1507 (ebook) | DDC 372.24/1--dc23/eng/20240123
LC record available at https://lccn.loc.gov/2023056892
LC ebook record available at https://lccn.loc.gov/2023056893

ISBN: 978-1-032-54950-7 (hbk)
ISBN: 978-1-032-54948-4 (pbk)
ISBN: 978-1-003-42823-7 (ebk)

DOI: 10.4324/9781003428237

Typeset in Galliard
by SPi Technologies India Pvt Ltd (Straive)

This book is for Maya, Jacobo and Jonah – their learning, their wellbeing and their future.

It is dedicated to them with radical love.

Contents

Acknowledgements   *xii*

Introduction   1

1 Agency: Power with, not power over   9

2 Safety: Physical, emotional, social, psychological and digital   26

3 Positivity: Strengths, solutions, smiles and support   45

4 Inclusion: Everyone welcome, everyone matters, everyone participates   71

5 Respect: For individuals, communities and human rights   90

6 Equity: Fairness and flexibility   107

7 ASPIRE in action across the world   131

Index   *140*

Acknowledgements

It has taken well over a decade to develop ASPIRE. During that time I have worked with schools, educators, researchers, families and communities, children and young people in many countries. For the most part they have deepened my belief in humanity, and that most want the best for young people and their future. Some have needed courage in the face of opposition from policymakers and others who have a vision for education that is not about wellbeing and learning for all, but about social control or building a business. I have learnt so much from them which has confirmed the validity and value of ASPIRE, not only in education but also in relationships – at home, at work and in our communities.

It is difficult to name everyone in this venture, but there are those without whom this book would not have seen the light of day. Foremost is my husband, David: proofreader, formatter, reference checker, indexer, techno adviser, tea-maker, comforter and travel agent. His support is integral to my own wellbeing, my thinking and my work. The rest of my family and close friends also deserve a mention as they keep me both grounded and uplifted!

Routledge Education is brilliant to work with and Alison Foyle, who has commissioned several of my books, is a star. Her belief in me and my approach to education has been a constant in this endeavour. I am immensely grateful.

I would like to also express my deep thanks for the willingness of so many to write about their experiences that illustrate the value of the principles. This is the strength of the book – being able to visualise examples of good practice throughout. All the ASPIRE principles are based in academic evidence, but they are brought alive by the stories that powerfully illustrate the difference they make to children, their teachers and the future.

Sue Roffey
October 2023

Introduction

This book addresses three interlinked questions:

- What is education for?
- What do we want for our children in school now?
- What sort of society do we want them to live in – and contribute to?

Do we want children to be curious about the world around them, excited by new discoveries, fascinated by all the possibilities for learning and keen to explore further, or do we just want them to get through the curriculum and cause as little trouble as possible? Of course, all pupils need to learn the basics in order to function in today's world, but there are ways to do this that promote an innate love of learning rather than stifle it.

Do we want a society that maximises the potential of all citizens and ensures everyone has what they need for optimal mental and physical health, and to live life with meaning, purpose and engagement? Or are we prepared to put up with increasing inequality, escalating unhappiness, deteriorating mental health, rising crime, misogyny, racism and corruption? If we want values of kindness, inclusion, fairness and respect for all to feature in our communities, this begins with the education we provide for our children and the relationships we have with their families.

Education is a means of preparing every child for the challenges of the 21st century, showing them how to engage fully with learning about the world around them and discriminate between what is real and what is not. Do we want students to have respect for science and evidence and be uplifted by creativity and innovation, or is education just a means to an economic end? Is education about the freedom for each child to become the best they can be or a means of social control? These are rarely absolutes, but the questions are relevant.

People talk about 'raising standards' in education as if the definition of education were a given. There is less discussion about 'raising engagement', let alone joy in learning. Education matters: what pupils are taught, how they are taught, and their experiences of the learning environment, are where children begin to discover all the possibilities of knowledge and understanding as well as who they can become, and how to build the relationships in which individuals, families and communities can thrive. In some countries this is happening. In others it is not, and the outcomes are seen in disaffection, disengagement, and despair for some and perhaps privilege for others – but not necessarily good mental health and a life well lived.

This book's title – *ASPIRE to Wellbeing and Learning for All in Early Years and Primary* – emphasises social justice. We are concerned about what is happening for all students in schools here and now, but also the future we are creating. What children and young people learn, both within and beyond the curriculum, shapes our world.

DOI: 10.4324/9781003428237-1

Beyond the pandemic

Covid-19 has had a profound impact on children, young people and their learning across the world. It has increased inequalities everywhere, and also highlighted many issues in education. Some children felt safer and happier at home, away from academic pressure, bullying and comparison with others; others became more vulnerable, as they were no longer monitored in a school setting. Although there was often the option of online learning, a concern for many was disconnection from their peers. This can be a cornerstone of resilience. Mental health has further deteriorated, and attendance in school has not returned to previous levels. There has been a 'catch-up' push from governments, but many organisations and educators have said that social and emotional wellbeing has to be a priority if children are to progress with learning. The impact of the pandemic may potentially affect a generation, especially for those already disadvantaged. This makes it even more vital that pupils feel welcomed, valued, connected, and accepted for who they are, that the curriculum is relevant and meaningful, and school is a place where children want to be.

Positive psychology

Traditional psychology aims to identify and analyse problems, with a view to developing effective treatments and interventions. Although there will always be a need for this, positive psychology has a different focus, in that it seeks proactive solutions that enable people to flourish and thrive. Rather than look for what is wrong and how we can fix it, positive psychology asks, "What do we know helps people become the best of themselves?" "How can we enable people to cope with the challenges life throws at them?" "What skills and attitudes promote authentic wellbeing?" and "What needs to happen so everyone has a chance of living well and contributing to the wellbeing of others?"

Positive education

Positive education emerged from the study of positive psychology and puts equal emphasis on wellbeing and learning – making connections between both. Children and young people make more progress in learning when they are experiencing a safe and inclusive school environment, and feeling good about themselves and their progress, other people and what is happening around them. This is not just about students, but also teachers, families and communities. Throughout the book we address the following:

- What would we see and hear in a healthy learning environment?
- What is already going well in terms of all children enjoying learning, feeling connected and making progress, and how might we get more of this?
- How can we align what happens in schools with what promotes healthy child development? This includes intrinsic motivation, a positive self-concept, and opportunities to explore, experiment, be creative and be challenged.
- What enables educators to be valued and respected for the vital roles they fulfil?
- How can education systems support families in their role, and promote the perceptions and competencies that enable children to flourish?
- What will ensure that children and young people of all abilities and from all communities, backgrounds and circumstances have both the educational approaches and resources they need to learn and thrive in education?

Wellbeing

Wellbeing is both complex and contextual (Street, 2018). It underpins not only mental health but also engagement with learning. The higher the level of wellbeing across a school, the more resilient the pupils, the more prosocial the behaviour, the greater the engagement of pupils, the better their achievements and the more teacher satisfaction (Noble et al., 2008).

Although many schools are doing their best, too many students, alongside teachers, are not having a good time in education. Wellbeing is still often reactive and takes place in silos rather than being proactive, comprehensive and universal – what happens for everyone, every day. This book aims to maximise a love for learning, build a positive sense of self, construct healthy relationships, foster resilience and help young people and educators make good choices. It also embraces the wellbeing of teachers and relationships with families.

There are many excellent texts on wellbeing and positive education, but for the most part they address issues separately, such as leadership, teacher wellbeing and behaviour. This book takes a different direction, and instead talks about how each of the ASPIRE principles need to be embedded through everything that happens in a school.

Learning for all

Although not acknowledged by every country, education has been recognised as a human right for all children across the world since 1948 (UNICEF, 2007). This is encapsulated in the United Nations Convention on the Rights of the Child (UNCROC), Article 28:

> *Every child has the right to an education. Primary education must be free and different forms of secondary education must be available to every child.*

There are references to other articles in UNCROC throughout the book, confirming that ASPIRE is integral to children's rights and how they should be treated in all circumstances, including in education.

There is significant evidence that the principles of ASPIRE impact positively on learning itself. The following is a quote from the UK Department of Education (2019):

> **Factors associated with countries high-performing education systems:** *Although a disparate array of factors is associated with the high performance of education systems in Estonia, Finland, Germany, Singapore and Taiwan, there are some common factors between these countries. These include: high levels of equity in educational outcomes/achievement (Estonia and Finland), teacher-quality (Finland and Singapore), support for pupils from disadvantaged populations (Finland and Taiwan) reform that promotes independent pupil learning, creativity and critical thinking (Singapore and Taiwan).*
>
> (Greatbatch & Tate, 2019, p. 3)

Ecological systems model

Positive psychology interventions in schools often make a difference for individuals. But what enables all in a school to thrive and learn is a critical ecological approach to wellbeing, and a recognition that this is not an 'add on' but a way of being. An adaptation of Bronfenbrenner's ecological systems theory helps visualise what this means (1979, 2004) (Figure 0.1).

The ecological systems model confirms that the most powerful influences on the developing child are at the micro-level: these are the interactions children have on a daily basis with those who care for them. In schools, this would be with teachers and peers. The words that

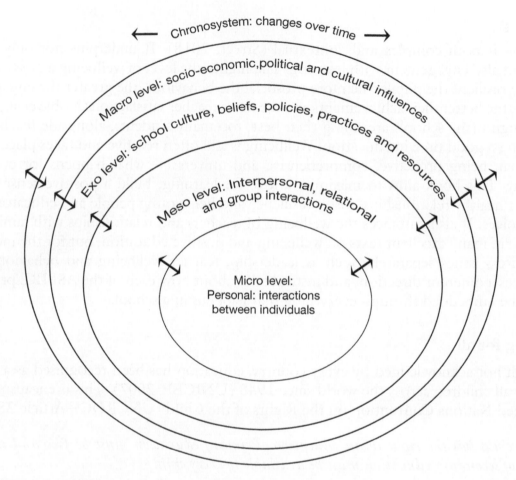

Figure 0.1 Ecological systems model (adapted from Bronfenbrenner).

teachers say to their pupils have a powerful impact on how they perceive themselves and the world of school. The quality of those interactions is embedded in what happens at the meso-level, which includes the relationships that these people have with each other. In families, this would be the relationship between parents, with extended family members, neighbours and those in the local community. In schools, it relates to relationships and conversations between teachers, staff and school leadership; what happens in classes; home-school interactions; and links with the local community. The exo-level for families is how workplaces and communities operate. In schools, this comprises the beliefs, policies and practices embedded in school culture, as well as the resources available. If a school's overriding priority is excellence in learning demonstrated by high grades, then the conversations between teachers will reflect that, and the interactions with pupils will focus primarily on their academic progress. At the macro-level are economic-socio-political influences. In the UK, this currently determines what is taught, how it is taught and the ways in which schools are inspected.

These systems, however, are not set in stone. Each level impacts bidirectionally on others. Teachers may feel they are controlled from above, but what they say and do can make a difference, not just for individual pupils but on the systems in which they work. The chrono-level in systems theory affirms that changes occur over time. Conversations create culture. They impact on what people believe, on how we position and treat each other, what matters, what we do and what is effective. Teachers change lives in more ways than they know.

What and why ASPIRE?

ASPIRE is an acronym for Agency, Safety, Positivity, Inclusion, Respect and Equity: together these encapsulate the principles underpinning positive education and wellbeing. They apply to everything that happens in a school, family and community. They have been developed over many years and are based in what we know about optimal child development; positive psychology; healthy relationships; a safe, strengths-based pedagogy; how children are motivated and learn; and healthy schools. The following is a brief synopsis.

Agency

Agency is power with rather than power over – it is the opposite of control, which is often toxic in a relationship. It incorporates self-determination, intrinsic motivation, self-directed learning, social action and the changing role of teachers in a digital age. Aligned with agency is responsibility, both individual and group. The chapter includes student voice and choice, stakeholder involvement in decision-making, and whole class responsibility for class culture. Agency is related to citizenship and future community engagement.

Safety

This incorporates physical, emotional, psychological and digital safety. Some children do not feel safe in school. The chapter includes the value of making mistakes, valuing diversity, reducing bullying, promoting collaboration over competition and the value of personal bests so that no pupil considers themselves a loser. We also give guidance on safe touch and digital safety.

Positivity

Negative feelings shut down cognitive pathways, so to maximise learning we need to promote the positive wherever possible. This includes using strengths-based language, a solution rather than problem focus, play and playfulness – often disregarded in education but valuable for mental health. This chapter outlines the micro-moments of positive action that foster kindness, optimism, gratitude and prosocial behaviour.

Inclusion

There is now a raft of research on the value of a sense of belonging for resilience and positive adaptation. This includes believing in the best of every pupil and students not only being valued but also being of value. Inclusion in school involves participation, progress with learning and having a recognised role. This chapter outlines the difference between inclusive and exclusive belonging and the importance of giving pupils opportunities to know each other, build connections and foster positive relationships: this goes beyond skill development to our perceptions and understanding of each other.

Respect

Respect is both for individuals and their ideas, but also for culture, not jumping to judgment without hearing, and understanding diverse stories. This requires good listening. Having cultural and contextual awareness means not imposing the dominant culture but taking account of community and context to promote active inclusion. Respect is demonstrated by adherence to the Golden Rule – treating others as you would have them treat you. We also consider respect for nature and the environment and for human rights.

Equity

Equity is aligned with fairness. There is discussion about 'levelling up,' but much less on how education systems might provide opportunities to do this. This requires flexibility, fairness and support. Equity also matters in the staffroom. This chapter looks at all the ways in which children have unique needs and concludes that education needs to be diverse. One size does not fit all. Equity is also about access to resources and the need to adapt the environment.

ASPIRE in action across the world

This chapter has case studies from Australia, China, the UK and South Africa putting all the ASPIRE principles into action and the difference this is making.

Although each principle is important in its own right and they are addressed separately in the chapters, they also interact with and reinforce each other. It is the application of all six principles across systems that promote optimal wellbeing and learning for all.

The structure of the chapters

Each chapter, except for the final one, has a similar structure. The first sections are the theory, rationale and evidence base for the principle, and the rest of the chapter is about putting this into practice with children, teachers, families and communities:

- What do we mean by the principle? – looking at definitions and applications
- Why does this matter? – including its relevance to wellbeing and learning and congruence with the UNCROC
- Putting this principle into practice in the early years
- Putting this principle into practice in the primary classroom
- Putting this principle into practice in the primary school
- Social and emotional learning
- A checklist
- Looking ahead – this principle in the future
- References and further reading
- Resources – including websites, podcasts, TED Talks and books for children.

Social and emotional learning (SEL)

UNESCO's four pillars of learning are learning to know, learning to do, learning to be and learning to live together (Delors et al., 1996). The first two are the knowledge and skills that have spurred innovation and development across the globe. We have a knowledge base that is truly extraordinary; the internet, space travel, and medical advances are just a few of the many projects that would be in the realm of magic and miracles a century or so ago. But we have not developed wisdom anything like as far or as well. The second two pillars are those needed for, amongst other things, strong, supportive relationships, conflict resolution and mental health, but have rarely had the same priority in educational settings. Learning to be and learning to live together are encompassed in SEL, which needs to be threaded through the curriculum as well as in targeted sessions. These need to happen in a safe, solution-focused space and the outcomes reinforced in everyday interactions. There are activities in every chapter that help children learn together about each principle and ways to action this in their lives.

As well as laying out the rationale for ASPIRE, each chapter showcases instances where these principles are happening and the difference this is making for stakeholders across a school. These case studies and vignettes provide powerful examples of the efficacy of ASPIRE internationally, and have been generously provided by students, teachers, school leaders, psychologists and academics.

Although the text is based in evidence, not everything is cited. This makes it more accessible to the reader. Those who want to know more are directed to the further reading.

Early years and primary settings

Learning begins the moment a child is born, if not before, and is at its most powerful in the first years of life when brain development is at its most rapid. Understanding and meeting a young child's social and emotional needs is critical, as this underpins engagement with learning. Promoting language skills gives children the tools for thinking as well as communicating, and there is now a stronger focus on oracy as both a prerequisite and extension to literacy.

Education systems need to be aligned with healthy child development. This includes the development of independence, opportunities to practice gross and fine motor skills, helping children learn to focus rather than react to multiple stimuli, developing and engaging social skills, learning through play, creativity and interactive games. It is the development of a positive sense of self and a curious, respectful approach to others. Positive liaison with families enhances both learning and prosocial behaviour. Families invariably want the best for their children and do the best they can with the knowledge, skills, resources and support available to them. Useful approaches that build positive partnerships are outlined in several chapters. The book addresses issues that often arise for primary-aged children, including relationships with peers, family changes and the inclusion of children with diverse needs.

Positive experiences underpin future mental health, and negative experiences undermine this. What happens in children's first and primary schools has implications for how they see themselves as learners and respond to learning opportunities. Preschools are ideal settings for attending to children's social-emotional needs, especially when this has been less than optimal at home. A focus on promoting strengths and a positive self-concept in primary schools, alongside giving children opportunities and encouragement to develop intrinsic motivation, enthusiasm for learning, and social and emotional competencies, can intervene positively in developmental trajectories.

It begins with belief

This book is admittedly idealistic, especially in the current climate. But this can also be seen as its strength. If we do not have a vision for a positive experience in schools for all children and their future, we risk staying with a reality that is clearly not working for everyone. We also know, as it is both cited and demonstrated here, that aspiring to ASPIRE is both possible and worthwhile. It begins with belief.

We need an education system fit for purpose for the 21st century, where all pupils thrive and make progress in learning and where wellbeing for everyone is at the heart of a school. Imagine what difference it would make when every child and young person wants to come to school, feels they matter when they are there, and develops confidence, resilience, curiosity about the world, a positive sense of self and healthy relationships. The evidence-based

ASPIRE principles of agency, safety, positivity, inclusion, respect and equity in practice can make that happen. This book shows how.

References, further reading and resources

Bronfenbrenner, U. (1979). *The Ecology of Human Development: Experiments by Nature and Design.* Harvard University Press.

Bronfenbrenner, U. (2004). *Making Human Beings Human: Bioecological Perspectives on. Human Development.* Sage Publications.

Delors, J. et al. (1996). *Learning: The Treasure Within; report to UNESCO of the International Commission on Education for the 21st Century.* UNESCO.

Greatbatch, D. & Tate, S. (2019). *School improvement systems in high performing countries.* Government Social Research, Department for Education.

Noble, T., McGrath, H., Roffey, S., & Rowling, L. (2008). *A Scoping Study on Student Wellbeing.* Department of Education, Employment & Workplace Relations (DEEWR) Australian Federal Government.

Street, H. (2018). *Contextual Wellbeing: Creating Positive Schools from the Inside Out.* Wise Solutions.

UNICEF (2007). *A Human Rights-Based Approach to Education for All.* United Nations Children's Fund.

Further reading

Bethune, A. (2018). *Wellbeing in the Primary Classroom: A practical guide to teaching happiness.* Bloomsbury.

Evans, K., Hoyle, T., Roberts, F. & Yusuf, B. (2022). *The Big Book of Whole School Wellbeing.* Corwin.

European Commission (2022). *Impacts of Covid on School Education.*

Giraldez-Hayes, A. & Burke, J. (2023). *Applied Positive School Psychology.* Routledge.

Grenville-Cleave, B., Guðmundsdóttir, D., Huppert, F., King, V., Roffey, D., Roffey, S. & de Vries, M. (2021). *Creating the World we Want to Live In: How Positive Psychology Can Build a Brighter Future.* Routledge.

Kern, M.L. & Wehmeyer, M.L. (2021). *Palgrave Handbook of Positive Education.*

Martineau, W. & Bakopoulou, I. (2023). What children need to flourish: insights from a qualitative study of children's mental health and wellbeing in the pandemic. *Education 3–13.*

Quinlan, D.M. & Hone, L.C. (2020). *The Educators' Guide to Whole-school Wellbeing: A Practical Guide to Getting Startedv, Best-practice Process and Effective Implementation.* Routledge.

Roffey, S. (2012). *Positive Relationships; Evidence based practice across the world.* Springer.

Roffey, S. (2020). *Circle Solutions for Student Wellbeing (3rd Ed.).* Corwin, Sage Publications

Sharp, C. & Nelson, J. (2021). *Recovering from Covid 19: What pupils and schools need now.* NFER Policy Briefing.

Sylvester, R. & Seldon, A. (Chairs) (2022). Times education commission report: Bringing out the best. *The Times.*

Resources

https://www.learning.nspcc.org.uk/child-health-development

1 Agency

Power with, not power over

What do we mean by Agency?

If we want children to become independent, active learners and participate positively in the world around them, we need to start early. Agency is the practice of giving children choices where possible, encouraging them to have a voice in what concerns them and also guiding them to think through the consequences of different actions, not just for themselves but for others. This enables them to have self-efficacy, a belief they can act – and that what they do has an impact and matters.

Agency and autonomy are often used interchangeably, as both mean being able to make your own decisions and not be controlled by others, but there is a significant difference. Autonomy is striving for your own goals and acting independently, regardless of what is going on around you. We see this in those who chose not to vaccinate against Covid-19 because of their values of personal freedom and not being told what to do. No-one, however, is entirely independent, as actions are influenced by others and the environment. Agency, on the other hand, is making decisions that take account of the context and that are often linked to influencing change and making a difference. We see this in people who did choose to be vaccinated against Covid-19 because this reduced the spread of the disease and protected everyone.

Ryan and Deci's self-determination theory (2000, 2018) has been significant worldwide in challenging the view that people only do things for external reward. The fulfilment of other innate needs matters. The theory comprises three linked components:

- Autonomy is the need for personal freedom to make decisions and be responsible for them.
- Competence is an individual's need to feel they have mastery over their social environment and outcomes.
- Relatedness is the need to feel a sense of belonging and connection to others.

This mirrors the concept of Agency we refer to here.

There are three dimensions to Agency:

- Having a sense of Agency: this is the belief that you can make decisions and affect change.
- Opportunities to exercise Agency: this will be dependent on context, especially relationships.
- The practice of Agency: this is the capacity and competencies to take action.

Children with a sense of Agency have a belief in their ability to make choices and that these will have consequences. They need to be given opportunities to put Agency into practice and have the skills to do so. Responses from others matter. Children learn from their earliest

DOI: 10.4324/9781003428237-2

experiences what happens when they choose to act and whether they were efficacious or not. This impacts on their sense of Agency in future similar situations.

Young children, for example, who are regularly faced with parental disapproval when they try to dress themselves, and even anger when they get things the wrong way round, may eventually become passive recipients of adult direction rather than strive for independence and self-efficacy. This also happens when caring parents do everything for their child rather than give them opportunities to try, fail, try again and succeed.

Similarly, if students are faced with a rigid curriculum with no room for creativity, innovation or the potential to influence change, they may not see themselves as having any ownership of their learning and perhaps not even try to become active, creative learners.

Children will inevitably have a stronger or weaker sense of Agency in different contexts and in relation with varying groups of people, more for instance with friends than with teachers.

Agency does not just apply to individuals but also to children acting together and in families, schools and other organisations. The social, cultural, economic and political context in which these exist determines the extent to which children are able to make decisions for themselves and how much they are listened to. This will also depend on what is available to them, especially within relationships.

Why does Agency matter?

Congruence with the United Nations Convention on the Rights of the Child

Article 12: Every child has the right to express their views, feelings and wishes in all matters
    affecting them, and to have their views considered and taken seriously.
Article 13: Every child must be free to express their thoughts and opinions.

These principles recognise children and young people as actors in their own lives and apply at all times throughout a child's life.

Agency is aligned with healthy child development, specifically independence and identity, psychological wellbeing, adaptation to adversity, intrinsic motivation, active learning and taking responsibility.

Healthy child development

Historically, children were regarded as passive 'human becomings' (Matthews, 2007) rather than as active agents in the process of development. However, a century ago, Piaget's theory positioned children as 'little scientists' observing and exploring their environment to gain understanding. This theory has been supported by a raft of evidence since.

Children are naturally curious, and when given opportunities to interact with the world will do so with enthusiasm. Adults may need to facilitate opportunities, but detailed direction is unnecessary. Though they do need to be available for the inevitable questions!

Children understand cause and effect from an early age. And as soon as they grasp that they can be 'causal agents', they begin to want to make things happen in their lives. Although a young child's determination to make their own choices can be infuriating, this drive towards independence needs to be recognised as a hallmark of healthy development.

There has been a good deal of research on parenting styles and their impact on the developing child (Baumrind, 1989; Mosco & O'Brian, 2012). Authoritative/facilitative parenting is warm and nurturing, but also provides structure, clear values, and high expectations. Facilitative parents are assertive about what is or is not acceptable social behaviour, and although this may involve setting boundaries, they also encourage independence, respect their child's autonomy, give them choices and provide them with freedom as well as support and guidance. This style has the best outcomes for children, who are positively attached to their family and grow to become independent, socially competent, active and confident adults. They also often do well academically. Schools that mirror the parenting style that facilitates healthy child development promote both wellbeing and learning.

Identity

When children have choices and efficacy, they are developing a sense of self – who they are, as well as what they can do. When these opportunities are not available, children may be conflicted and lack confidence. They are likely to have low self-worth and not able to feel proud of who they are becoming. Children are all different, and who they become reveals itself over time, like different plants in a garden. Without the freedom to explore and make choices for themselves, their identity may never fully blossom. They will always be relying on others to tell them what to do and how to be.

When these individuals become adults, they may be in positions of authority over others. They are likely to stay with what they have already been told, perhaps because it feels familiar and safe. They may maintain the status quo rather than attempt to initiate or change anything. This can lead to organisations becoming 'stuck' rather than innovative.

Wellbeing

Self-determination is now accepted as one of the central pillars of psychological wellbeing (Ryan & Deci, 2018). The satisfaction of the basic psychological needs of autonomy, competence and relatedness promotes healthy functioning at all levels of human development and across different cultures and settings. Martela and colleagues (2022) found that these needs were aligned with wellbeing across 27 European countries strongly associated with happiness, life satisfaction, meaning, and lack of depressive symptoms.

When these basic needs are not met, optimal development and positive engagement with the world is frustrated. Children who are routinely controlled by others, either by over-protection or by authoritarian approaches, do not have this basic tenet of wellbeing. Things happen to them rather than with them. It may be hard to stay optimistic, motivated and engaged if you feel that nothing you do makes any difference. It is also harder to develop personal strategies to cope with adversity when you always look to others to tell you what to do.

Taking responsibility

Once you give someone Agency, they take responsibility for outcomes, whether these are positive or not. If a project is successful, they can rightly feel proud – but if it goes wrong, there is no one else to blame. When others are in control, it is easy to lay the blame there. Many teachers will have come across pupils who quickly say, "It was them, not me", when something problematic occurs in the classroom or playground. These are often children who have not had enough experience of Agency and the important element of accepting and learning from mistakes.

Intrinsic motivation

Motivation is the driver for action. It is what gives people the energy to do things. Many believe that people only do things for reward – the more you pay someone, the better their performance; the better your exam results, the more your parents and teachers will be pleased. This is extrinsic motivation.

Self-determination theory challenges this view and says that meeting psychological needs is more powerful. People often choose to do things because they are interested in them and enjoy doing them. Sometimes this fits with their values, such as action on climate, or because they want to get better at something – like playing a musical instrument, developing skills in a sport or learning a language. This is intrinsic motivation.

The drive to explore, experiment and push limits to get better at things, is powerful. The political economist Dan Pink (2018) illustrates in his research how often people choose to do things for no external reward, because it has meaning for them in either personal development or community contribution. It gives them eudaemonic happiness – the feeling they are living a good life.

There are many studies which suggest that children who are intrinsically motivated are better at learning. In fact, intrinsic motivation is often indicated as one of the most powerful predictors of academic achievement. It is aligned with self-directed learning.

Active learning

From the time they are born, children are active self-directed learners. They engage with the world around them by observing, exploring, interacting, trying things out, sorting, creating and using their imagination. When they have sufficient language, their learning includes asking questions and making up stories.

I once heard a politician say that without teachers, children would not learn anything, and I wondered if he had ever had the opportunity to spend any time with children. Perhaps he meant that they would not learn what he wanted them to learn!

Agency is aligned with engagement, and children who are fully engaged in what they are doing will be absorbing knowledge.

Agency in education

According to the OECD (2019), Agency in education is about *"acting rather than being acted upon; shaping rather than being shaped; and making responsible decisions and choices rather than accepting those determined by others"*. When children are routinely told what to do and how to do it, they not only miss out on learning vital life skills, but they also are unable to build on their own interests, strengths and concerns.

Traditionally, education is teacher-directed. Agency in education is giving young people more ownership of their learning rather than invariably dictating what they should be doing, how and when.

In school, children may learn that their own choices of activities and their own judgments of competence don't count; what matters are the teachers' choices and judgments. The goal in class, in the minds of many students, is not competence and understanding but good grades. A system of constant testing and evaluation in school – which in some countries becomes increasingly intense with every passing year – is a system that substitutes extrinsic rewards and goals for intrinsic ones. It is almost designed to produce anxiety and depression in those whose achievements are not deemed worthy of celebration.

Agency is central to learner identity, autonomy and behaviour. Giving children a sense of Agency needs to be matched by empowering them to take ownership of their learning. When opportunities are provided for pupils to exercise their Agency in relation to various aspects of the learning process, they acquire effective control. Making opportunities explicit and readily accessible enables all students to recognise and tap into their potential.

Agency is not just about pedagogy but also the curriculum. What children learn about themselves, the world around them and their place in it is configured by curriculum content.

Children can change the world

When my eldest daughter was 5 years old my wife and I watched with awe as she diligently put together an illustrated booklet about climate change and posted it to Theresa May, the prime minister at the time. This began a journey as a change-maker that included more letters to politicians, sponsored events for animal charities and fundraisers in support of those affected by the war in Ukraine.

We saw first-hand the double benefit of children engaging in social action – benefiting both the causes they were supporting, and also our children themselves, who developed a sense of Agency, empathy, leadership, and enhanced well-being. We learnt of the long-term benefits of engaging children in social action from an early age, with research finding that children involved in meaningful giving by the age of 10 are more than twice as likely to make it a lifelong habit.

Yet, when it comes to social action in schools, children are rarely given Agency as to which causes they support or the activity they carry out. This inspired a journey to build a platform to educate, inspire, and empower children everywhere in taking action for the world around them. The platform, www.superkind.org, offers child-safe coverage of important problems in the world, inspirational case studies of over 50 young change-makers, and step-by-step toolkits for how to take different actions. We also work with educators to curate a series of lesson and assembly plans so social action can easily and meaningfully be integrated into school life.

Children can change the world. Not just one day in the future but right now.

Keren Mitchell

When students are positioned as empty vessels to be filled with information that is regurgitated at appropriate moments, the direction of learning is a one-way street. This is not only disrespectful to students and their prior knowledge, but also far from reality. Pupils have information, understanding, ideas and experiences that colour and position new knowledge, so it makes sense for learning to be interactive and build on what students bring.

Without Agency, young people may begin to think that things just happen to them and they are incapable of influencing anything. It becomes easy to blame others for anything that goes wrong. They may be anxious and reluctant to take the initiative. They may also get bored when everything is teacher-driven and their own interests, concerns and strengths are not taken into account in the classroom.

Agency as a principle enhances wellbeing and engagement with education, and builds a society where citizens see themselves as potential agents of change.

Agency in practice in the early years

Young children rarely have the same external expectations placed on them that older students do. There are no tests hanging over them, and although early years educators will have criteria to aim for, children are not told they have to meet targets and judged on whether they have 'passed' or not. There are potentially plenty of opportunities for children to direct their own learning – usually through play. However, where there are external expectations placed on early years educators to get children 'ready for school' the freedom to explore without clear direction or purpose might be compromised.

Agency is contextual: circumstances matter. This is especially critical for younger children, who may be pushing boundaries to establish their independence. Freedom to assert control does not mean they can do as they please all the time. This undermines their sense of security and can be overwhelming, as well as being unrealistic for parents and educators.

The National Quality Framework (NQF) in Australia was set up in 2012 to regulate early learning and school-age care. This specifically highlights Agency as a key concept to a child's development:

- **NQF Outcome 1.2** – Children develop their autonomy, interdependence, resilience and sense of agency.
- **NQS 1.1.6** – Each child's agency is promoted, enabling them to make choices and decisions and to influence events and their world.

The UK non-statutory guidance for the early years foundation stage, *Development Matters* (2021), does not mention agency as a guiding principle but does refer to the importance of independent learning and how adults can support and extend this:

- Children need opportunities to develop their own play and independent exploration. This is enjoyable and motivating.
- Young children's learning is often driven by their interests. Plans need to be flexible.
- Three characteristics of effective teaching and learning are:
  - Playing and exploring – children investigate and experience things and 'have a go'
  - Active learning – children concentrate and keep on trying if they encounter difficulties, and enjoy achievements
  - Creating and thinking critically – children have and develop their own ideas, make links between ideas, and develop strategies for doing things
- Sometimes (practitioners) make time and space available for children to invent their own play. Sometimes, they join in to sensitively support and extend children's learning.

Agentic learning in an early years setting will be different for each child. Learning through play is not routinely setting out activities for children to complete but giving children freedom and encouragement to follow their own interests, whether this be dinosaurs, guinea pigs or rockets. Facilitating this depends on adults observing and listening to children, asking questions and following up, perhaps suggesting joint activities where children have the same curiosity.

Interests don't come from a totally blank canvas. Although some children will have a stimulating home life, not all do. Early years educators present children with a wide range of experiences and ideas, from stories, picture books, outings, puzzles, nature and animal activities, arts, crafts, music, physical challenges, and much more. Conversations that emanate from these stimuli help children to develop language and the tools for thinking, including developing imagination. This extends engagement with play, both solitary and with others. When children follow their own pathways to learning, this becomes deeper and broader and more likely to be remembered.

Adults need to be in charge of the environment without controlling children. For instance, an early years educator aiming for children to develop an understanding of number may put out a selection of toys and activities that support this and will be there to make suggestions and answer questions. This is different from giving children a choice from all the toys in the centre or insisting they complete a given task.

Small children are often resistant to direction. Unless, of course, the child has already learnt to be passive. Some individuals, despite many external controls, will thrive, especially if there are people around who believe in them and respect their right and ability to make their own decisions. A teacher is often that person.

Agency in practice in the primary classroom

Self-directed learning

Most adult learning is self-directed. People read books, search for information on the internet, join a class or a group with the aim of achieving something and practice a skill to get better at it. But how does this translate into teaching approaches in a primary classroom so that children become lifelong learners? Van Deur and Murray-Harvey (2005) explored the practice in six Australian primary schools. They found that successful implementation was dependent on both internal and external factors. These interact with each other, with some being dependent on children's earlier experiences.

Internal factors:

- The task being presented to children needs to stimulate their interest, creativity and critical thinking.
- Personal characteristics of self-motivated learners include a belief they can do it, willingness to make the effort and coping strategies to keep going when things are challenging.
- Personal learning strategies include planning, checking and reflecting on what is being achieved.

External factors:

- The school context, where student Agency is valued
- Opportunities in the class for enquiry and taking responsibility
- Teacher guidance and coaching, including explicit strategies for self-directed learning
- Classroom organisation, including collaborative learning
- Resources – books, IT, other people.

The following case study shows how interest was stimulated, motivation developed, and opportunities presented to children. The example here comprises the highlights of a much more extensive project.

Answering the Calls – Ecole Laura Secord School (E.L.S.S), Canada

The Canadian Truth and Reconciliation Commission (TRC) was established in 2008 as a way of informing both indigenous and non-indigenous people across the country about what happened in Indian Residential Schools, and how the legacy of that still impacts today. The final report in 2015 concluded that such abuses of indigenous peoples were deliberate acts of cultural genocide. This is defined as the forcible removal of culture and traditions from a minority group through legislation, education, and social conditioning so they lose their identity as a people. The TRC published 94 Calls to Action to promote reconciliation in the key areas of child welfare, education, language and culture, health, and justice.

In 2017, as there was no forthcoming 'child-friendly version' of the 94 Calls, several educators in Winnipeg invited students from years 4, 5 and 6 at E.L.S.S. to reword the 94 Calls in a language children could understand. This project began by exploring pre-colonial life on Turtle Island, researching what it was like for inhabitants there. They then visited the Canadian Museum for Human Rights, where they were saddened and outraged by what they learned about colonisation. With the support of an indigenous activist and educator, the children then learned about the purpose of the TRC and that the 94 Calls were intended to be a practical guide to reconciliation in a country that needed healing. Following an activity that demonstrated the importance of clear instructions, the children were challenged to capture the essence of the often wordy 94 Calls and find the 'ah-ha' meanings. These were illustrated in poems and pictures. The following is a selection of the 'sound poems' addressing child welfare, education, language and culture, health and justice.

- Keep families together, safe to provide family healing (Sloan F.)
- Eliminate discrepancy in education funding for First Nations Children (Blair J.K.)
- Help promote all Aboriginal languages (Benji W.)
- Close the gaps in Aboriginal and non-Aboriginal Health (Micah D. and Jalyan D.M.)
- Governments cannot defend actions of historical abuse (Allie J.)

The section on Reconciliation includes the following:

- Fully adopt the United Nations Declaration on the Rights of Indigenous People (Grace P.)
- We call upon the church to respect the Rights of Indigenous Peoples
- Maintain commitment to Aboriginal education, Kindergarten to Grade Twelve Learn Aboriginal history and legacy of residential schools. Build understanding, sympathy, respect. Religious studies much include Aboriginal beliefs (Lilly S.)

The children then reworded each of the Calls in child-friendly language, writing instructions for action on each one. You can read this substantive work in *Answering the Calls: A Child's View of the 94 Calls to Action* (Churman et al., 2019).

Agency in practice across the primary school

Children's willingness and ability to be active and productive members of their communities is often underestimated. Given opportunities, guidance and support to explore, collaborate and take action, pupils can both contribute to social change and develop positive skills, attitudes and self-concept in the process.

> *Youth social action is happening every day in schools around the country and educators are going the extra mile to provide civic learning opportunities for their pupils.*
>
> (Gunn et al., 2023)

Teachers do not always recognise that raising money for charities, doing sponsored walks or having community events comes under the umbrella of social action and do not necessarily see this as a valuable tool for learning and wellbeing. They are inhibited from making youth social action a central platform of school culture because of a perceived lack of time and resources to make it happen. But projects do not have to be elaborate or large scale to be meaningful and can often support the curriculum.

Youth social action

The Royal Society of Arts (RSA) is committed to a world where everyone can fulfil their potential and contribute to more resilient, rebalanced and regenerative futures.

As part of this endeavour, the RSA, with funding support from the Pears #Iwill fund, the National Lottery, and the Department for Culture, Media and Sport, initiated youth social action projects in ten primary schools across England. They outline the factors that enable social action to be effective and high quality:

- Pupils have ownership over the goal and the means of the youth social action project
- Pupils feel connected to their local community and part of something bigger
- Pupils perceive that the project is sufficiently difficult, including feeling a sense of 'controlled discomfort'
- Pupils feel that the project is successful
- Pupils are supported to recognise their personal development.

Schools can foster a culture that encourages pupil voice and also be connected and engaged with their local community. Although students need to be able to lead, shape and own their projects, it is useful to link these with the curriculum wherever possible so that the learning is embedded across different subjects. Having milestones increases commitment and accountability – knowing what success would look like at different stages of the project.

Not only do pupils and communities benefit from social action but staff do as well.

"Building a learning environment that is infused with trust and co-Agency provides the very best foundations for lifelong learning" (Alison Peacock).

Here is a small selection of the projects the schools were involved with:

- St Bernard's Roman Catholic School in Cheshire partnered with Chester Zoo to focus on the songbird crisis in Indonesia, where songbirds are suffering from loss of habitat and illegal trade. They raised awareness in various music and drama projects, leafletting and letter writing.
- Queensmead Primary Academy, Leicester, partnered with several organisations to embed youth social action at different school levels. This included improving the school environment, planting trees around the playground and overhauling the school's recycling policy. Other groups have linked with local care homes to practice their reading with residents. During the pandemic they became pen pals. One of the acknowledged benefits of youth social action has been building stronger connections with parents who may become involved in the projects with their children.
- University of Cambridge Primary School has projects running every half term. One whole-school, cross-curricular project focused on the experience of refugees, centring around Francesca Sanna's book *The Journey*. Pupils were inspired to create an 'around the world' dance in their PE lessons and later developed fundraising activities for a local refugee charity.

Roger Hart's ladder of participation (1992, 2008) is a way of thinking through the extent to which children's participation is authentic. This metaphorical ladder has eight rungs, with each ascending level giving children increasing decision-making, control and power.

The lowest levels are manipulation, decoration and tokenism, to the highest level, where child-initiated decisions are shared with adults.

Kids Against Plastic

Kids Against Plastic is an inspiring youth-led environmental charity that aims to combat the menace of plastic pollution and climate change. My sister Ella and I founded the charity when we were ten and twelve years old, after reading about the UN's sustainable development goals which inspired us to take action. We were shocked by what we learned, and wanted to spread the information to others and encourage everyone to make a small difference.

At its core, KAP is about empowering young people to take action. The charity aims to educate and mobilise children and teenagers to understand the gravity of plastic pollution and climate change, and to embrace sustainable practices both at home and in school, for a better planet.

Kids Against Plastic has two educational initiatives: the Plastic Clever Schools initiative focuses on reducing plastic pollution and promoting sustainability in educational institutions; Climate Clever Schools aims to educate students about climate change and encourage environmentally friendly practices in schools to mitigate its impact. Numerous schools nationwide and around the world have registered for both initiatives thereby inspiring thousands of school children to take action and have an impact on their environment.

The Kids Against Plastic Club boasts over 190 members who engage in various activities. Weekly Zoom meetings, led by us, Amy and Ella, serve as a platform for learning about environmental issues and participating in themed activities. Members are encouraged to partake in litter picks, earning badges and certificates for their efforts. We are also proud to work alongside individual members who lead campaigns such as picking up a million pieces of plastic litter and writing to supermarkets asking them to stop selling children's comics that are covered in 'plastic tat'.

My sister and I are passionate environmental activists who want to inspire fellow young people to stand up, take action and make a difference. We strongly believe that young people are the future and can make a huge difference now.

Amy Meek, Co-founder and CEO, Kids Against Plastic, www.kidsagainstplastic.co.uk

There is a spectrum in every school between total adult control to pupils making their own decisions about what works best in their context. This includes what is taught, how it is taught, expectations on teacher time and what is prioritised in school policies.

Teacher–student relationships

Agency in primary schools is facilitated or inhibited by the actions, decisions and beliefs of the adults. This principle is about empowerment – power *with* rather than power *over* – and is the opposite of control, which is invariably toxic in any relationship. Relationships between teachers and students are already unequal, because a teacher has more power than a student. Using this authority to empower pupils is more likely to promote positive behaviour and engagement with learning than asserting power and being authoritarian.

A common discourse on teacher-student relationships is that a 'good' teacher has to be in control of their students, and if they are not chaos will ensue. There are stories in the media about 'out of control' schools, often with a call for 'more discipline'.

A healthy relationship, however, is where there is equality and shared decision-making. A controlling and coercive relationship is now recognised in UK law as toxic and dangerous. Overbearing control in schools does not model positive relationship skills and undermines protective factors in resilience. It is also exhausting, and can lead to resentment, reducing rather than increasing the chance of prosocial behaviour. Where pupils are already emotionally volatile it can spark a meltdown. At the far end of controlling relationships, we find bullying and abuse.

In many schools, however, teachers have to deliver a curriculum and get pupils through tests to show what they have learnt. They may feel that the only way to do this is to establish high levels of control. Many children may accept this, as they want to please teachers, get good grades, or not get into trouble, but this approach may both undermine a pupil's engagement with a subject and impact negatively on their wellbeing. This is as true for the compliant students as it is for the disruptive ones.

What can teachers do instead when they are pulled in two directions – maintaining/raising educational outcomes and giving students a voice and choice? There is a difference between being in charge of proceedings in a class and controlling students. A teacher who is able to be in charge of proceedings in the classroom, orchestrate events, lead, support, guide, encourage participation, provide timely feedback, and be responsive to individuals as well as the group, does not need to control students. An effective educator encourages self-control and believes in the ability of students to learn this and put responsibility back where it belongs.

Relationships are enacted by what is said and not said and messages that are given about value and expectations. Words are powerful. They can be used for positive effect but also have the potential for damage.

Glasser (1998) says external control is destructive to relationships and that being disconnected is the source of almost all human problems. He advocates seven caring habits to counter what he calls 'deadly habits' which undermine healthy relationships:

Example of a practical application in school:

Deadly habit	Caring habit	Example
Criticising	Supporting	"How can I help you?"
Blaming	Encouraging	"Tomorrow is another day; let's try again then."
Complaining	Listening	"What happened? What did you want to happen?"
Threatening	Trusting	"I will come back later and see how you have got on."
Nagging	Accepting	"That didn't go well. How can we move on and make this better?"
Punishing	Respecting	"The decision is yours, but you need to know the consequences."
Bribing – rewarding to control	Negotiating difference	"Let's see if we can both get what we want here."

For intrinsic motivation to flourish pupils must feel free to take risks with their learning, and be innovative in responding to challenges, knowing they have the permission, support and respect of their teachers.

Behaviour

There is a concern in the UK and elsewhere that pupil behaviour is worsening – especially since the pandemic. Teachers often struggle with children who have poor concentration, little emotional regulation and are not compliant. Unfortunately, many educators still believe that a behaviourist approach is the way to go. Although it might have immediate impact, it is unlikely to change behaviour beyond the moment, and the same behaviours are likely to re-occur. For our most distressed pupils, whatever sanctions are imposed will not come close to what they are already dealing with. And if we focus on tangible rewards for good behaviour, children may begin to expect such rewards for compliance.

Behaviourist approaches are based on the premise that people only do things out of fear of punishment or for tangible reward. This promotes extrinsic motivation, where pupils learn behaviour 'from the outside in'. Behaviour 'from the inside out' is where children make their own decisions because it makes them feel good about themselves and promotes a sense of belonging. This will not be effective if children already feel alienated. Feeling good might include getting your own back. Fostering inclusion is linked to prosocial behaviour.

Teachers have to deal with behaviour in the moment it is occurring, but also need to consider what works in the longer term so they don't keep reinventing the wheel. Positive changes are more likely to occur when strategies and approaches are cohesive and focus on an agentic approach.

It is useful to find out what is going on for pupils and what this means for them, and giving them choices about the way forward.

Here are some phrases that might be useful. Bear in mind that children who are in a high state of emotion will not be able to think straight, so they will need to have space to calm down first. This also gives teachers a moment they might need to gather their thoughts.

- What was going on there? Can you tell me what happened?
- You were hurting other people – that is not on - what could you do instead to show how angry/upset you are?
- What went wrong? It is OK to make mistakes because we learn from them. Is there anything you have learnt from this?
- I am at a loss to know how to help here – do you have any ideas?
- Could you draw how you are feeling/what would help?

Teacher Agency

Many teachers are struggling with educational policies that undermine their voice and choice. It is one reason staff are choosing to leave the profession. It is, however, possible to increase teacher Agency when the senior leadership team maximises consultation. One teacher in a research project told me that she understood that the school executive had to make final decisions, but her support for these depended on whether or not she felt genuinely consulted. Having things imposed from above can lead to resentment and subversion. It is not only what happens in schools that matters but how they happen. Using a Circle Solutions format, all staff can engage in discussions about new policies and procedures. This process gives everyone a voice and helps prevent the louder and more confident voices becoming dominant in decision-making.

Whole staff consultation

- The issue is introduced by a member of the senior leadership team, often as a question or challenge to be resolved.
- Everyone is mixed up so that cliques are disbanded.
- Staff work in pairs – or a three if there is an uneven number.

- Partners are given 5–10 minutes to discuss the positives and negatives of the issue, including what is already working well and whether the new initiative aligns with the school's vision.
- After 5 minutes they join with another pair to see what they have in common.
- Each group of four reports what they share, and this is written up for everyone to see.
- This stays up until the next staff meeting to give time for reflection.
- At the next staff meeting, people are again mixed up into groups of four, and the staff executive ask for specific input on the issue based on the earlier discussion. This is where opinions are turned into action and policy. Feedback from each group informs the leadership team, who then make final decisions taking account of what has been said.
- Policies are reviewed after a term and tweaked where necessary, using the same format.

Agency in social and emotional learning (SEL)

Agency is demonstrated in SEL when pupils come to their own decisions about values and behaviours rather than being told by those in authority. Activities are presented as games, hypotheticals, discussions and reflections that enable children to think through important issues in their lives in a safe place. Most of the time, there are no right or wrong answers, but children will have had the opportunity to talk with others and reflect on alternative ways of being and living together.

Activities in SEL

Strengths in Circles Cards:

There are seven statements for each of the six ASPIRE principles.
   These are three of those for Agency:

* We give things a go.
* We have choice.
* We use our strengths.

In groups of three or four, students take one statement at a time and discuss the following questions together:

– What does this mean?
– Is this what we want in our class?
– What would it make people feel about being here?
– What help do we need?
– Is it already happening – how do we know?
– What else might we do?

Each group decides on one action. They give a brief report back to the Circle, emphasising the action. What they all agree is put on display as a reminder.

Choosing who to be:

You may choose to give students a heads-up about this activity, so they have time to think about it. Doing the same activity year on year shows children that their ideas of what is important change as they get older and more mature.

Go around the Circle giving students the name of a sport – football, swimming, skateboarding, running, high jump. You ask everyone to change places until everyone has had a turn. Pupils then partner with someone next to them. You can also do this with fruit, colours, animals or numbers.

Now pupils pair up to talk with each other. These paired interviews take place in different Circles, but all are intended to focus children on personal characteristics and values. The teacher also takes part so they will know when to swap over/end the activity.

Discussion 1: Do you have a role model – who do you look up to and why? This can be someone you know personally, a fictional character or someone famous.

Discussion 2: If you could be any animal, what would you choose and why?

Discussion 3: If you could have one superpower, what would that be and why?

Each person listens carefully so they can report on their partner's choice. If there is feedback to the whole Circle, each pupil needs to check with their partner if they are comfortable with that or would prefer to pass.

Hypotheticals:

Discussions take place in small groups with presentations to the whole Circle.

First, mix students up so that they work in random groups.

1 Community action

Imagine someone has left some money to your school. About as much as a teacher's yearly salary. Each group is a committee responsible for spending this in the best possible way. What would make the most difference to the most pupils?

1st Circle: Each group discusses ideas and decides on the project they want to pursue.

2nd Circle: Planning and making a presentation to the rest of the Circle

3rd Circle: Each group presents their ideas to the whole Circle to persuade others theirs is the best. There is then a vote.

Students might like to think about how they might get this action off the ground in reality, beginning with checking out what budget they would need and where to apply for funds.

2 Choosing a charity

The class is preparing to do some fundraising for a charity. Each group considers which area is of most interest to them and they want to work for: the list can include but is not limited to the following: health, refugees, children, homelessness, animals, environment, the aged or human rights. The groups make a case for their chosen charity and present to the class, who vote for this. This activity can, of course, be taken further as a whole class project deciding on what actions to take to raise funds.

Agency checklist

	This is in place – we know it is effective because...	*Working on it – our actions to date are...*	*Just started – our next step will be...*
Pupils spend part of the day in self-directed learning and know how to do this			
Pupils are given opportunities to explore and report on interests			
Pupils are encouraged to evaluate their own progress and identify achievements and next steps			
Teachers understand the difference between being in charge of proceedings and controlling students			
Teachers are consulted on policy and practice			
Social action is part of school culture			

Agency in the future

For a healthy, democratic society, we need active, engaged, responsible citizens who know that they have a voice and can effect change. It is not only knowledge that they need, but also confidence and ability to work in teams. Young people collaborating with others to make thoughtful decisions can influence positive change and development from a school to a community to a global level. In order to do this, they must learn to evaluate information, take initiatives, apply their learning, and be able to problem-solve. We underestimate pupils and their potential if we see them as simply absorbing and then regurgitating information passed on by others, rather than active and interactive in the process of critiquing, understanding and applying knowledge. Unless they have opportunities to have Agency and make a difference when young, they may not learn these vital skills, and become dependent on others to create the world they live in.

References, further reading and resources

Baumrind, D. (1989). Rearing competent children. In M. Damon (Ed.), *Child Development Today and Tomorrow*. Jossey-Bass.

Churman, R., Cleave, J., Cotton, C.B., Joanette, J. & Jones, S. (2019). *Answering the Calls: A Child's View of the 94 Calls to Action*. Ecole Laura Secord School, Winnipeg.

Department for Education (UK). (2021). *Development Matters: Non-statutory guidance for the early years foundation stage*.

Dept of Education, Australian Federal Government. (2023). *National Quality Framework*. https://www.education.gov.au/early-childhood/national-quality-framework

Glasser, W. (1998). *Choice theory: A new psychology of personal freedom*. Harper Collins.

Gunn, N., Daly, A. & Tejani, M. (2023). *Make it Authentic: Teachers Experiences of Youth Social Action in Primary Schools*. Royal Society of Arts.

Hart, R.A. (1992). *Children's participation: From tokenism to citizenship*. United Nations Children's Fund International Child Development Centre.

Hart, R.A. (2008). Stepping back from 'the ladder': Reflections on a model of participatory work with children. In A. Reid, B.B. Jensen, J. Nikel & V. Simovska (Eds.), *Participation and Learning: Perspectives on education and the environment, health and sustainability* (19–31). Springer.

Martela, F., Lehmus-Sun, A., Parker, P.D., Pessi, A.B. & Ryan, R.M. (2022). Needs and wellbeing across Europe. Basic psychological needs are closely connected with wellbeing, meaning and symptoms of depression in 27 European countries. *Social Psychological and Personality Science*, 1–14.

Matthews, S.H. (2007). A window on the 'new' sociology of childhood. *Sociology Compass*, 1(1), 322–334.

Mosco, J. & O'Brian, K. (2012). Positive Parent-Child Relationships. In S. Roffey (Ed.) *Positive Relationships, Evidence-based practice across the world*. Springer.

OECD. (2019). *Future of Education and Skills 2030 A Conceptual Framework Student Agency for 2030*. https://www.oecd.org/education/2030-project/teaching-and-learning/learning/student-agency/Student_Agency_for_2030_concept_note.pdf

Piaget, J., & Cook, M.T. (1952). *The origins of intelligence in children*. International University Press.

Pink, D.H. (2010). *RSA Animate: Dan Pink – the surprising truth about what motivates us*. https://www.youtube.com/watch?v=u6XAPnuFjJc

Pink, D.H. (2018). *Drive: The surprising truth about what motivates us*. Cannongate Publishers.

Ryan, R.M. & Deci, E.L. (2000). Self-determination theory and the facilitation of intrinsic motivation, social development, and well-being. *American Psychologist*, 55(1), 68–78.

Ryan, R.M. & Deci, E.L. (2018). *Self-Determination Theory: Basic Psychological Needs in Motivation, Development and Wellness*. Guildford Press. [An introductory sample chapter is available online. https://www.guilford.com/excerpts/ryan.pdf?t=1]

Sanna, F. (2016). *The Journey*. Flying Eye.

Van Deur, P.A. & Murray-Harvey, R. (2005). The inquiry nature of primary schools and students' self-directed learning knowledge. *International Education Journal*, 5(5), 166–177.

Other sources and further reading

Arthur, J., Harrison, T., Taylor-Collins, E. & Moller, F. (2017). *A Habit of Service: The Factors that sustain service in young people.* University of Birmingham: The Jubilee Centre for Character & Values.

Bandura, A. (2008). An Agentic Perspective on Positive Psychology. In S.J. Lopez (Ed.), *Positive Psychology: Exploring the Best in People Vol 1 Human Strengths* (167–196). Praeger.

Body, A., Lau, E. & Josephidou, J. (2019). *Our charitable children: Engaging children in charities and charitable giving.* University of Kent.

Body, A., Lau, E. & Josephidou, J. (2020). Engaging children in meaningful charity: Opening-up the spaces within which children learn to give. *Children & Society, 34*(3).

Gurdal, S. & Sorbring, E. (2018). Children's Agency in parent–child, teacher–pupil and peer relationship contexts, *International Journal of Qualitative Studies on Health and Well-being, 13:sup1.*

Roffey, S. (2019). *The Primary Behaviour Cookbook.* Routledge.

Sirkko, R., Kyrönlampi, T. & Puroila, A.M. (2019). Children's agency: Opportunities and constraints. *IJEC, 51,* 283–300.

Sorbring, E. & Kuczynski, L. (2018). Children's Agency in the family, in school and in society: implications for health and well-being. *International Journal of Qualitative Studies on Health and Well-being, 13:sup1.* [This is the introduction to a special edition of the journal. All papers are open access.]

Twenge, J.M., Zhang, L. & Im, C. (2004). It's beyond my control: A cross-temporal meta-analysis of increasing externality in locus of control, 1960–2002. *Personality and Social Psychology Review, 8,* 308–319.

Wehmeyer, M.L., Hyeson Cheon, S., Lee, Y. & Silver, M. (2021). Self-Determination in Positive Education. In M.L. Kern & M.L. Wehmeyer (Eds.), *The Palgrave Book of Positive Education.* Palgrave Macmillan.

Resources

Agency in Action; Chartered College: https://www.my.chartered.college/impact_article/pupil-agency-in-action-developing-curriculum-and-pedagogy/

OECD Student Agency for 2030: https://www.oecd.org/education/2030-project/teaching-and-learning/learning/student-Agency/

Make it Authentic: Teacher's Experiences of Youth Social Action in Primary Schools: https://www.thersa.org/globalassets/_foundation/new-site-blocks-and-images/reports/2023/07/make-it-authentic-2023.pdf

Citizens of Now: High Quality Youth Action in Primary Schools: https://www.thersa.org/reports/citizens-of-now-high-quality-youth-social-action-in-primary-schools

Roger Hart's Ladder of Participation: https://www.organizingengagement.org/models/ladder-of-childrens-participation/

https://www.superkind.org A free platform for schools to bring social action and philanthropy into the classroom.

2 Safety

Physical, emotional, social, psychological and digital

What do we mean by Safety?

There are grim stories about how some schools operated in the past – and not just in fiction. They were places of cruelty where pupils were brutalised by staff and expected to bully and intimidate each other. Punishments were harsh and meted out for a wide variety of misdemeanours. Children who 'couldn't take it' and showed distress were ridiculed. Pupils learned to shut down feelings for themselves and for others. Empathy and kindness were considered 'soft', and it was not so much the survival of the fittest but the survival of the meanest – especially for boys. This was not just in schools for local children but also in more privileged echelons of society, where families sent their children away as young as 7 to get a 'good education'. We see the impact of such regimes in the attitudes and behaviour of some people today who believe that 'strong discipline' is the way to get children to 'behave' and that positive relationships are not a feature of an effective classroom. They are not interested in the evidence that says otherwise, because their educational experience "didn't hurt me" – except that it did, in ways they may not fathom. They may have learnt ancient history, classics and calculus, but they didn't learn about love, positive connection, healthy relationships and authentic wellbeing. Unless, of course, they had exceptional teachers looking out for them and providing role models.

Although all schools now have safeguarding procedures in place, Safety across the learning environment is much more than policy documents. It is included here as a positive education principle because children need to feel safe at school in order to thrive and learn. Evidence suggests that pupils may have a less positive view of Safety in their school than staff do – so it is worth checking in with them.

Safety is physical, social, psychological, digital and emotional, and there are overlaps between these. Physical Safety means a learning environment that children can explore without seriously harming themselves or others, and where they can trust people to keep an eye on them. Social Safety means acceptance and support from peers, while psychological Safety is freedom from fear of violence, harassment, bullying and intimidation, both actual and witnessed. Digital Safety includes not being exposed to dangerously misleading, coercive or threatening material online, and knowing how to keep yourself and others free from harm. Emotional Safety is being able to maintain a positive sense of self by not being humiliated, rejected or negatively labelled.

Safety in school is where pupils are accepted for themselves and free to learn, communicate, ask questions and seek help without fear of punishment, and do not need to be hypervigilant in case someone attacks them, either physically or verbally. Feelings of Safety are not generally enhanced by barbed wire, armed guards or a set of rules beginning 'don't', but by a sense of positive community where everyone matters and feels supported and cared for.

DOI: 10.4324/9781003428237-3

Why does Safety matter?

Congruence with the United Nations Convention on the Rights of the Child

Article 3: The best interests of the child must be a priority in all decisions and actions that affect children.

Article 19: Protection from violence, abuse and neglect. Governments must do all they can to ensure that children are protected from all forms of violence, abuse, neglect and bad treatment by their parents or anyone else who looks after them.

Children who feel safe at school are more likely to be able to concentrate and learn. Positive emotions foster creativity and problem-solving, whereas anxiety shuts down cognitive pathways and impedes attention.

Children need to be able to trust that the adults around them have their best interests at heart. Every child should feel safe with their teachers. If a pupil is worried about what will happen if they make mistakes, they may resist making an effort or taking risks with their learning. This limits their knowledge and understanding and undermines attainment. When educators are so focused on results that they do not have the time or resources to find out what would help those who are struggling, children may not feel safe in school.

Children need confidence to play and explore freely. Insecurity may make them more likely to stay with what is familiar and comfortable rather than seeking challenges and mastery. This may limit their physical and social development.

Insecurity inhibits social relationships – children may be wary or even scared of others. This can lead to children being friendless and perhaps isolated, which is a risk to their mental health and wellbeing.

Bullying in school can have far-reaching consequences for both the bully and the bullied. When children are routinely put down, ridiculed, intimidated, ganged up on, pushed around, excluded and disempowered, they feel useless, helpless, scared and generally unsafe. They may develop both physical and psychological problems that can last into adulthood. It is one of the main reasons children opt out of school. Children who bully may be at risk of further antisocial behaviour, addictions and family violence, although this also aligns with the experiences that may have led them to bully in the first place, such as aggressive role models and/or lack of emotional support. Children who witness bullying behaviour at school can also have anxiety, depression and poor attendance.

For some pupils the fear of going to school may be overwhelming. This can result in doing everything they can to stay home. Persistent absence from school may lead to increased vulnerability, disadvantage and negative life trajectories. Outcomes, however, depend on the personal characteristics of the pupils, the reasons for their absence and the support from home. Punitive measures are counterproductive. See the chapter on Inclusion for more on this.

UK Safeguarding Procedures

In the UK, there are published guidelines about what schools should do to protect children from maltreatment, prevent the impairment of their physical or mental health and development, ensure children have safe and effective care and take action to ensure they have the best outcomes. There is an emphasis on early identification of potential abuse or neglect, whether that is for young or older students, and the document includes a list of issues that are likely to make children more at risk, such as being a young carer, being disabled, having an education, health and care plan, being persistently absent from school or living with family members who are coping with addiction, imprisonment or violence.

Safeguarding and promoting the welfare of children is everyone's responsibility. Everyone who comes into contact with children and their families has a role to play. In order to fulfil this responsibility effectively, all practitioners should make sure their approach is child centred. This means that they should consider, at all times, what is in the best interests of the child.

(DfE, 2022)

Schools have to appoint a designated safeguarding lead, responsible for ensuring teachers are aware of potential issues for pupils, responding to concerns that are raised and liaising with others in the community, such as social services.

Although much in the guidance is positive and supportive and is a concerted attempt to stop children falling between the cracks, concern has been expressed over the extent of paperwork involved, and a view that safeguarding in some schools has become a tick-box activity that meets inspection requirements, rather than an authentic child-centred response to need and the establishment of a safe, warm and respectful learning environment. There is also a lack of confidence that the requirement to report suspected abuse will be followed up promptly, as there are not enough personnel in social service departments to do this. Concerns about children's Safety have risen since the pandemic, with many students not returning to school.

Australian Safe Schools Framework

In Australia the focus on Safety is more proactive and strongly aligned with wellbeing for all:

All Australian schools are safe, supportive and respectful teaching and learning communities that promote student wellbeing.

The Framework identifies nine key elements to assist schools in planning, implementing and maintaining a safe, supportive and protective learning community that promotes student Safety and wellbeing. These are:

1 Leadership commitment to a safe school
2 A supportive and connected school culture
3 Policies and procedures
4 Professional learning
5 Positive behaviour management
6 Engagement, skill development and safe school curriculum
7 A focus on student wellbeing and student ownership
8 Early intervention and targeted support
9 Partnerships with families and community.

These are the components of element 6:

6.1 A strong focus on the enhancement of student engagement with learning.
6.2 The extensive use of cooperative learning and other relational teaching strategies.
6.3 Teaching of skills and understandings to promote cyber Safety and for countering harassment, aggression, violence and bullying.
6.4 Teaching of skills and understandings related to personal Safety and protective behaviours.
6.5 Teaching of social and emotional skills (e.g. listening, negotiation, sharing, empathic responding) in all subjects and across all year levels.

Details of all other elements are found on the website listed in the references at the end of this chapter.

Safety in practice in the early years

It is a significant moment for many parents when they leave their child in the care of an early years teacher – they need to know that they will be safe and cared for. But early years professionals also know that children need to explore and sometimes push boundaries, so this can be a balancing act.

There are several aspects to physical Safety in early years settings.

1 Reducing accidental risk by keeping dangerous items away from children. No one thinks that having sharp objects within reach of little fingers is a good idea – but children also need to learn how to use implements safely, so there are now knives and scissors designed for this purpose.
2 Giving children opportunities to make good decisions to stay safe outside and in the playground. If you watch young children in a park, they are constantly checking out the parameters of what is and is not possible. They might bump into each other sometimes or even walk under a swing, but for the most part they interact safely both with equipment and with other children. Without this practice they do not learn the skills they need to assess situations and make good choices. Soft surfaces reduce the chance of injury if they should fall.
3 Everyone in the community is responsible for children's wellbeing and Safety – without telling them to be careful all the time! Children are everyone's business.
4 When risk evaluation has taken place, specific policies can be developed which give everyone guidance on both everyday Safety procedures, including hygiene, and emergency situations, such as floods, fire or violence. This also applies to primary schools.

Emotional Safety is equally as important for young children, as coming to an early years provision means leaving their primary carer, perhaps for the first time. Both parent and child need reassurance, as emotions are contagious and an adult can be more upset than their child, making it harder for everyone. The calmer the adults are able to be, the easier it is for the child. Giving children permission to cry and explaining why they might feel that way is a step on the way to emotional regulation, a critically important skill. Young children might also find a transitional object useful for a while, something they bring from home that they can hold close and comforts them, such as a soft toy or blanket. Most young children quickly learn to trust the adults in an early years setting and feel safe with them, especially their keyworker, who makes the effort to discover and value their unique character, strengths, interests and needs.

Safety in practice in the primary classroom

Physical Safety in school is critical to protect children who are more vulnerable. This could include pupils born with specific difficulties who need a supported environment, those who have temporary needs such as broken bones and those who have chronic illnesses including diabetes, coeliac, asthma and allergies. This last is now a serious issue in schools with a huge rise in dangerous reactions to specific foods, insect stings and substances such as aspirin and latex. An anaphylactic attack caused by ingesting an allergen either through the mouth or skin can be fatal without rapid action. All adults in a school need to know what to do.

Good practice saves lives

In Australia, every staffroom has photographs of children with allergies, with information about the different substances they are allergic to. Every teacher knows which students are at risk and from what. They know what the symptoms of an anaphylactic attack are so can take immediate action. There are adrenaline auto-injectors (epi-pens) in every classroom, and teachers have been trained how to use them in the event of an emergency. This saves lives and needs to be replicated in every school everywhere.

Teacher-pupil relationships: building trust and Safety

Predictability

Children naturally look to the adults in their lives to provide security and predictability. Unless they have already been let down badly, children are invariably trusting. When this trust is broken it can take a while for them to feel safe with anyone.

Consistency and reliability

When adults are reliable and consistent they build and maintain trust. This includes being careful of what they say and only promising what can be delivered. Routine is also important, so pupils can predict what is going to happen and develop competence in understanding expectations. When changes in routine are signalled clearly and in good time children have more chance to adapt, and not be alarmed by the unexpected. Even minor transitions are particularly challenging for children who are neurodiverse, so they need good notice of these.

Kindness

This is encapsulated in what is said to pupils. When conversations are warm, strengths-based and encouraging, children may lose the fear of being ridiculed or demeaned. This is especially important for those whose behaviour reflects unsafe experiences elsewhere.

Being listened to

Children need to know that they will be listened to and taken seriously. When they feel secure in the people around them they are able to confide concerns and ask for help when they need it. It is not always easy for busy teachers to attend to one child when there are many other things going on in the class, but when pupils know that their teacher will be available they can wait until then. Although pupils need to be assured that what they say will not be shared widely, they cannot be told that it will be kept confidential if they or someone else is at risk of being hurt.

Getting attention

In my first teaching job with young children, I was told "the quieter you are, the quieter the children will be". This has proved to have validity across all ages. Some children have been shouted at most of their lives and have learnt to ignore what is being said. When an adult raises their voice at a pupil, however, it is not only the target child who may be affected but the others around them, including some who may be easily alarmed. It is also not an effective way of reducing problematic behaviour – the children hear the volume of the voice rather than the words being spoken, and if this happens often, they may begin to take no notice.

Getting children's attention by visual strategies, however, can be very effective. Just putting a hand up and expecting everyone to do the same, look at you and stop talking is one way. Putting a finger on your nose and expecting children to do the same – with the last person having to snort like a pig is another! The laughter releases tension and promotes connection.

Teaching and learning

A safe learning environment enables students to take risks and try things out, ask questions, and seek help when needed. Safety in learning is complex and aligned with a sense of self. Many pupils have such a focus on perfection that they never feel good enough. Others don't make an effort because they see themselves as failures – and never feel good enough! Schools can raise motivation and Safety in learning by changing language, reducing individual comparisons, and promoting collaboration over competition.

Language

Comment on what has been achieved, however small. Then ask what the student will do next. Praise effort rather than ability. Self-evaluation is also useful, as this promotes intrinsic motivation and encourages students to take on learning challenges.

Personal bests

Pupils understand this concept from sport. Once someone is competing against themselves they are never a loser – and more likely to value their own progress.

Cooperative learning

When students are working together they will learn from each other both in research and discussion. One of their tasks could be to devise questions to ask about a topic. See the chapter on Agency for more on this.

Safety in numbers

Some students are embarrassed by being put on the spot in a class, even if they know the answer. When a question is opened up to all, it is the dominant and confident pupils who quickly put their hands up. Using the Circle Solutions strategy of asking students to discuss an answer in pairs not only relieves anxiety for some, but it also gives more pupils opportunities to have a voice.

Mistakes

When these are acknowledged as a stage in learning, pupils will be less reluctant to have a go. Using scaffolding and steps towards completion or a task also helps. All writers know the value of drafts and critique. Children can also understand this concept.

Practice

Not many of us can master a skill the first time around. Opportunities to practice are valuable – especially when they can be positioned as games. This might be the role of homework.

Celebration

Many schools only celebrate sporting and academic achievement, but learning is about all the UNESCO four pillars: learning to know, learning to do, learning to be and learning to live together. Celebrating all of these gives them credibility and more children a chance to shine.

Safety in practice in the primary school

Growing good men

There have been multiple stories in the media about misogyny in various public services and the danger to women and girls that emanates from this. Much of the focus has been on vetting new recruits, but every one of the men who hold these views has been a boy who went to school. If we want a society free of toxic masculinity, then what happens in the learning environment matters. This is not only important for the future Safety of women and girls but also for the wellbeing of boys and men, their own mental health and the health of their relationships. We need to think about how boys grow into good men who are proud, not ashamed of their gender.

Schools can take actions that increase gendered Safety for everyone.

- Positive role models can be powerful, not only male teachers but also men who have qualities that boys often admire, such as sporting prowess, who also demonstrate qualities of character and are outspoken about respect for women.
- Activities that are not stereotyped by gender so that both girls and boys are offered the same opportunities to develop interests and skills.
- Challenging statements that exonerate unacceptable behaviour such as 'boys will be boys'.
- Avoiding the suppression of emotion, such as 'boys don't cry' or 'get a grip'.
- Helping all students to understand the biology of emotion and discuss the skills of emotional regulation and the importance of attaining this.
- Stories that challenge the typical 'male hero' strong man and offer alternatives for how to be.
- Providing opportunities for structured conversations about relationships/friendships, including issues of consent.

There is more on this issue in the Secondary version of this book.

Safety and consent

Children from a young age need awareness of their rights to self-protection and have pro-active conversations about consent. It can, however, be hard to initiate these important discussions with children, and adults are not always clear about their own responsibilities in keeping children safe. The following is an Australian resource that addresses both.

Safer Communities for Children

Safer Communities for Children is a program offered in Australia by the National Association for Prevention of Child Abuse and Neglect (NAPCAN). It is an inclusive, culturally safe, whole-of-community protective behaviours approach, specifically designed for young children aged from around 4 to 8 years. The approach utilises beautifully illustrated bush animal stories with specific messages about Safety that particularly reinforce the responsibility of adults to value and keep children safe. It also aims to elicit the voices of children on what makes them feel safe and encourages adults to respond in ways that are meaningful and relevant for their children and community.

Safer Communities for Children offers a new approach to protective behaviours in that it:

- is a primary prevention approach that focuses on children's rights and wellbeing
- seeks to encourage Agency and give children a voice in their own Safety
- focuses on raising community awareness of every adult's role in protecting and supporting children, and
- provides practical strategies for parents, services and communities to hear from children about what makes them feel safe and to create physically and emotionally safe environments that promote children's Safety and wellbeing.

Safe touch

Media coverage of sexual abuse of children by adults who are supposed to care for them has led to a fear of being accused of inappropriate touching, and many teachers will stay well away from a child, even when that pupil is in need of physical reassurance. Many also have real concerns about what to do when a child is out of control, despite government guidelines on restraint. It is a dilemma for many, so this safe touch policy, developed by John Ray Junior School in Essex, is a thoughtful and helpful response. It is too long to replicate in full, but these are the relevant paragraphs:

John Ray Junior School: Safe Touch and Positive Handling Policy

Children learn who they are and how the world is by forming relationships with people and things around them. The quality of a child's relationship with significant adults is vital to their healthy development and emotional health and wellbeing.

Our policy takes into account the extensive neurobiological research and studies relating to attachment theory and child development that identify safe touch as a positive contribution to brain development, mental health and the development of social skills.

At John Ray Junior School, we have adopted an informed, evidence based decision to allow safe touch as a developmentally appropriate intervention that will aid healthy growth and learning. Our policy rests on the belief that every member of staff needs to know the difference between appropriate and inappropriate touch and can demonstrate a clear understanding of the difference. Equally, when a child is in deep distress, staff are trained to know when and how sufficient connection and psychological holding can be provided without touching.

Different Types of Touch:
There are five different types of physical contact that may be used:

1. Casual/Informal/Incidental Touch:
Staff use touch with pupils as part of a normal relationship, for example, comforting a child, giving reassurance and congratulating. This might include putting an arm out to bar an exit from a room, taking a child by the hand, patting on the back or putting an arm around the shoulders. The benefit of this action is often proactive and can prevent a situation from escalating.

2. *General Reparative Touch:*

This is used by staff working with children who are having difficulties with their emotions. Healthy emotional development requires safe touch as a means of calming, soothing and containing distress for a frightened, angry or sad child. Touch used to regulate a child's emotions triggers the release of the calming chemical oxytocin in the body. Reparative touch may include stroking a back, squeezing an arm, rocking gently, cuddling, tickling, sitting on an adult's lap, or hand or foot massage.

3. *Contact Play:*

Contact play is used by staff adopting a role similar to a parent in a healthy child-parent relationship. This will only take place when the child has developed a trusting relationship with the adult and when they feel completely comfortable and at ease with this type of contact. Contact play may include an adult chasing and catching the child or an adult and child playing a game of building towers with their hands.

4. *Interactive Play (Rough and Tumble Play):*

This structured play follows clear rules and is operated under close supervision by staff. It will only ever take place when all participants are in agreement and completely understand the rules. This sort of play releases the following chemicals in the brain:

- Opioids – to calm and soothe and give pleasure;
- Dopamine – to focus, be alert and concentrate.
- Interactive play may include: throwing cushions each other or using soft foam bats to 'fence' each other.

5. *Positive Handling (Calming a Dysregulating Child):*

Trained staff will restrain a child when behaviour is:

- Unacceptably threatening, dangerous, aggressive or out of control;
- In order to avoid harm to self or others or damage to property;
- To avoid an offence being committed and/or a breakdown of good order and discipline.

A child who is in a state of dysregulation and has no mechanism for self-calming or regulating their strong emotional reactions will be physically contained by staff. This kind of containment will usually involve a member of staff sitting behind the child and enveloping the child in their arms whilst providing a safe, calm and soothing presence. It may also be necessary for another member of staff to control a child's kicking legs. Staff will employ the safest and gentlest means of holding a child, which is entirely designed to enable the child to feel safe and soothed and bring him or her down from an uncontrollable state of hyper arousal. During any incident of restraint, staff must seek as far as possible to:

- Lower the child's level of anxiety during the restraint by continually offering verbal reassurance and avoiding generating fear of injury in the child;
- Cause minimum level of restriction of movement of limbs consistent with the danger of injury (so, for example, will not restrict the movement of the child's legs when they are on the ground unless in an enclosed space where flailing legs are likely to be injured);
- Ensure at least one other member of staff is present.

The following actions should be taken before a restraint is used:

- Conversation, distraction, coaxing skills, gentle persuasion or redirection to other activities (e.g. touching the child's arm and leading him / her away from danger, gently stroking the child's shoulder);
- Encourage the child to help him/herself feel more secure by wrapping a blanket tightly around him/herself or holding on tightly to a large cushion or stuffed toy;
- Put distance between the child and others – move others to a safer place;
- Calmly remove anything that could be used as a weapon, including hot drinks, objects, furniture;
- To prevent a child continuing to pose harm in a dangerous situation, advise others to leave, but remain with the child yourself;
- Use seclusion only if necessary for a short period while waiting for help, preferably where a member of staff can observe the child;
- Keep talking calmly to the child, explain what is happening and why, how it can stop, and what will happen next;

Use first aid procedures in the event of injury or physical distress when safe to do so.

Behaviour

When children have experienced conflict, rejection and/or trauma, they are often alert to potential negativity in their environment – their default position is not to feel safe. This means that their amygdala – the organ in the brain that reacts to perceived threat – will be triggered by anything that bears any, even faint, resemblance to earlier events. When the amygdala goes into action, it prepares the body to fight, freeze or flee. Instructions from the brain to do this are rapid – much faster than the neocortex, the thinking part of the brain. This means that reasoning with children in an 'amygdala moment' is not viable. Others need to do one or more of the following:

- Minimise perceived threat by standing back from the child and not invading their personal space. Keeping hands down also helps.
- Keep voice low and slow.
- Acknowledge and validate the emotion being expressed – this shows the child that their distress has been 'heard', and may reduce the need to express it more forcefully.
- Where possible, give an instruction to do something, not stop something – it's easier for children to comply.
- Keep others away from potential fallout.
- When possible, suggest the child moves to a quiet space.
- Show care and comfort, and do not ask 'why'.
- Once the child has calmed it may be helpful to ask, "What happened to make you so upset?" Do not press for an answer if that is not easily forthcoming.

Safety from bullying

The biggest threat to Safety in school is bullying. Evidence suggests that one in five children experience this on a daily basis, more in primary than secondary schools (Long et al., 2020). Bullying is not a one-off incident of aggression but repeated acts of verbal and physical intimidation, manipulation, humiliation, exclusion and other micro-cruelties that are perpetrated by one or more pupils who see themselves as wielding power over a less confident peer, often a child who is different in some way from others, perhaps with a disability or specific ethnicity. It is invariably supported, either overtly or covertly, by others who may be fearful that they will be the next target or want to feel powerful themselves. The outcome for children who are bullied can be severe and include depression, anxiety, sleeping and eating difficulties, low self-esteem, poor self-worth, helplessness, refusal to come to school and loneliness. Cyberbullying can mean that there is no escape, even when at home. Bullying also negatively affects those who witness this behaviour because it reduces their own feelings of Safety in school.

Anti-bullying policies are often reactive to perpetrators, usually imposing sanctions. It may be that children are bullying others because this is happening to them, so punishment may not change this behaviour over the longer term. If they are being hurt at home, involving parents may exacerbate this. Responses need to be sensitive, with consideration for the potential consequences. Sometimes the focus is on the children who are bullied, showing them ways to cope and what to do if they find themselves being intimidated, such as walking away. This is useful, but it takes courage and might be risky. We have to think differently.

Bullying can only really thrive in a culture that turns a blind eye. More than anything, children need support from others in a school that generates empathy, together with practices that make it more difficult for bullying behaviour to be swept under the carpet. I once asked primary-aged children about the extent of bullying in their school. They had a no-put-down policy, and everyone knew what that meant because it had been part of whole-school conversation. Making fun of someone or making them feel bad was just unacceptable.

Bullying can be effectively addressed by actively promoting inclusion, generating empathy and exploring whole class support. See the social and emotional learning section at the end of this chapter.

Digital Safety

Online Safety is an increasing concern, as many children now have access to devices that put them at risk. They need to be aware of the dangers and how to protect themselves from an early age.

Mighty heroes

This is an excellent resource for younger primary-aged children. It consists of four animated videos and teacher notes for each. Each of the videos showcases an Australian animal with a superpower that promotes online Safety.

- Wanda the Echidna has the superpower of responsibility. They talk about protecting personal information.
- River the Super glider has the power of respect. They talk about how some people are unkind and mean online, so it is important to be encouraging and respectful instead.
- Billy the Bilby has the superpower of investigation. They check in with information that is posted to see if it is real or not.
- Dusty the Frilled Neck Lizard has the superpower of trusting their feelings. Sometimes feelings suggest that you step away from things that might be dangerous. Not all 'friends' online are trustworthy – they might not even be children.

Teacher Safety

Most educators want positive interactions with families and do their best to foster these. There are times, however, when teacher Safety is at stake when adults arrive at school in a rage. There are ways to handle this that de-escalate confrontation, maximise Safety and do not damage future relationships.

If the individual is drunk or under the influence of drugs, call for the assistance of another member of staff and suggest the person leaves. You may like to say that you will make an appointment to see them when you can have a constructive conversation. Ask when a good time for them would be to meet with you. Perhaps suggest that they bring a partner or friend to support them. It is also possible that the person is having a breakdown. The same applies, as you cannot resolve any concern in such circumstances.

If the family member is sober but angry, invite them into a classroom or office and ask them to sit down. It is harder to maintain fury when seated. Take a chair yourself near an open door and then use active listening skills until their rage has run its course. Going on the defensive is never useful, so wherever you can, validate their concerns. When they run out of steam, say something positive about their child and that you are pleased they have taken the trouble to come and talk with you. This may help them appreciate that you both want the best for this pupil and you would like to sort out their issue. Reassure them that they know their child best – this positions them as the expert and will reduce the power imbalance that may be at the heart of their aggression. Some parents may feel that unless they shout and scream at someone in authority they are not heard, and nothing gets resolved. This may be how they have experienced issues in the past. Use a solution-focused framework that explores what a resolution would look like for them and then give the pros and cons of various options, including whether their ideas are feasible and in line with school policies. Decide on a plan where possible, and agree on a review date so that the parent knows you are on their side.

Teacher Safety in the staffroom is similar to pupil Safety in the classroom. I once worked with senior academics who were intimidated in faculty meetings. The leadership team dominated all decisions. Unless you were part of a favoured team of acolytes, your opinion was unwanted and any contribution to discussion consequently belittled. This toxic environment undermined trust and coloured conversations, and good people left. Safety needs to be threaded through the entire school system to enable everyone to give their best.

Healthy child development and risk-taking

Some adults believe that children need to be kept safe at all costs and put in restrictions that prevent them not only from exploring but also from learning how to keep themselves safe and balance risk with challenges. When children are restricted and controlled by adults in this way, they are more likely to become teenagers who are less able to think for themselves and make good judgments about indulging in risky behaviours.

Most children naturally want to have a go at things; they want to explore not only their environment but also test out their own limits. They have an innate drive towards mastery. As children follow their curiosity and try new things, they are developing neural connections that foster understanding and confidence. It is vital that the adults around children not only provide guidance but also encouragement, especially when they are not successful in their first attempts at something.

Learning to make good judgments is part of healthy development. A child who is checking out the balance of risk and danger when climbing is learning about space, testing out the strength or fragility of objects, planning moves and exploring the parameters of their physicality. We live in a world that is increasingly risk averse, and this can have an impact on how children develop and learn (Gill, 2007).

Safety in social and emotional learning (SEL)

Safety can be compromised in SEL if pupils are invited to talk about personal issues and feelings in a public forum. This can risk discomfort, embarrassment or anxiety for students and a worry for teachers who may not have the time, resources or training to respond effectively with sensitivity during the session, although all disclosures of harm need to be followed up as soon as possible. It is crucial that students have opportunities to discuss, reflect on and make decisions about ways of being, but they need to do this in a secure environment. Safety in Circle Solutions is maintained in several ways:

- Almost all activities take place in pairs, small groups and the whole Circle. There is no individual competition.
- There is the right to 'pass'. No one has to speak if they choose not to. Respecting this decision means not going back to anyone individually by name to encourage a contribution. Children often want to please teachers and may find themselves in conflict. The teacher may, however, ask the whole Circle if anyone has now thought of something they wish to say.
- The focus is on issues, never incidents. Pupils are regularly provided with opportunities to discuss hypothetical situations. This enables issues to be addressed in impersonal ways that do not risk breaching confidentiality.
- There is no naming or blaming.
- The use of the third person rather than first, such as replacing 'I' and 'me' and 'my' with 'someone' or an abstract term. Instead of "It makes me happy when…", a safer sentence completion is "It would make someone happy if…" or "Happiness is…" Although children are likely to say things that refer to themselves, they are not expected to.

Activities in SEL

Bullying is a concern in many schools, and there are often anti-bullying policies in place aimed at identifying those who bully and placing sanctions on them. Although this may have an immediate impact on increasing Safety within a specific context, it is not a sustainable solution. There is also advice on what individual pupils might do if they are being bullied. But bullying can only thrive where the culture supports it. Developing a safe and friendly class where everyone takes responsibility for the wellbeing of each other is more effective over time. Here are some ways to do this.

Building a safe and friendly class

> **Pair share and sentence completion:**
>
> Pupils are mixed up, and then work with a partner to talk about why Safety at school is important and what needs to happen to make sure everyone feels safe. They then complete the sentence going round the Circle:
>
> - Safety in school means …
> - We feel safe in school when …
>
> They may need to be reminded that there is no naming or blaming in Circles.

Group design:

Pupils work in groups of three or four to design a safe and friendly class. They are given a large piece of paper that they can draw and write on. Each person in the group contributes. They are asked to show what people would see in a safe and friendly class, what they would hear and what everyone would be feeling. Ten minutes for this activity should be sufficient. Each group shows and explains their design to the whole Circle. When everyone has done this, the teacher highlights similarities between them.

Strengths in Circles Cards:

There are seven statements for each of the six ASPIRE principles.
These are four of those for Safety:

* We are kind in what we say and do.
* We look out for each other.
* We learn from our mistakes.
* We can get help.

In groups of three or four, all students take one of these statements and discuss the following questions together.

– What does this mean?
– Is this what we want in our class?
– What would it make people feel about being here?
– Is it already happening – how do we know?
– What else might we do?

Each group decides on one action. They give a brief report back to the Circle, emphasising the action. What they all agree is put on display as a reminder.

Trust

Trust is often an abstract concept, but thinking it through with others in Circles is a way of increasing relational Safety in a class. Spreading these activities over several weeks maintains a focus on the issues raised and builds good practice in class.

Mix pupils up with these silent statements:

– Everyone who knows what it means to trust someone change places.
– Everyone who knows what it means to be trustworthy change places.
– Everyone who thinks that trust is a good thing to have in this class change places.

Sentence completions:

In pairs, pupils discuss how they will finish this sentence stems:

– You know you can trust someone when …

They agree on two sentence completions, and each pupil says one of these going round the Circle. It is OK if people say the same things as it shows what everyone thinks. The teacher points out what has been said most often.

Mix pupils up again and ask them to complete these sentences:

– Being able to trust other people would make someone feel …
– Not being able to trust someone would make people feel …

Small group discussion for older pupils.

If Trust walked into our classroom tomorrow morning:

– What would we notice? What would be different?
– What might we see, hear, think and feel?
– What could we do to make sure Trust stays?

Each group has three minutes to tell the rest of the Circle what they would notice and what actions might be needed to increase Trust in their class.

Hypotheticals:

A student volunteers to read out a brief story about a pupil in a particular situation. This is one about someone who is not feeling safe at school. The story is always in the first person, which is fine because it is fictional – though the issues are not. The teacher may need to amend the story so that it does not identify anyone in the class.

My name is Sami. I was born with a red mark over my face, but otherwise I am just like other students. I am good at running and I love reading. But there are some kids in my year who pick on me and call out things like "here comes the traffic light", and some of them have begun to push me around in the playground. I wish it would stop.

The pupils work in groups of three or four. They are asked these questions one at a time.

– How would you feel if you were Sami?
– What would you want to happen?
– What is one thing this group could do to help?
– Who will do what when?
– What do you need to make this work properly and ensure everyone is safe?

Someone from each group comes up to Sami and asks if their action plan is something he would like to happen to help make him safe.

There are many more hypotheticals in *Circle Solutions for Student Wellbeing* 3rd Ed (2020), addressing such issues as racism, disability and children in different families.

Upstanding:

Show the video in the resources and ask children to discuss in pairs the sorts of things they might do to stop bullying – which one of the four options in the video might they try. These are:

* Be a buddy
* Interrupt
* Speak out
* Tell someone

Now ask them what they might say:

– To someone who is being bullied
– To the person who is bullying

The class now has some ideas of how to stop bullying in their class and make school a safer place to be. When strategies have been developed by pupils themselves rather than being told by a teacher they are more likely to put them into action.

Safety checklist

	This is in place – we know it is effective because …	*Working on it – our actions to date are …*	*Just started – our next step will be …*
Pupils' views on how safe they feel at school			
Staff views on school Safety			
Staff know what to do in a medical emergency			
Mistakes positioned as a necessary step in learning			
Child-centred approach to Safety procedures			
Safe touch policies in place			
Focus on developing friendly, kind and inclusive classrooms			
Pupils encouraged to be 'upstanders' to bullying			
Curriculum input on digital Safety			
Staff given trauma-informed training			

Safety in the future

Our children are growing up in a world that in some ways is safer than ever before. Child mortality in many countries is much lower than in previous eras, and we have more or less eradicated a number of serious illnesses, such as polio, smallpox and diphtheria. But the Covid-19 pandemic shows that without vigilance and collaboration these advances in physical Safety may not be sustainable.

Children are increasingly unhappy and for many their emotional Safety is fragile, with more pupils experiencing anxiety, depression and low self-esteem and with some resorting to self-harm. Mental health concerns increase with age, but many begin while children are at primary school.

When families are stressed by poverty and isolation, they may not have the resources to ensure the wellbeing of their children. There are record numbers of children at risk of abuse and neglect, and many witness family conflict and violence even when not hurt themselves. Some are refugees and asylum seekers who have experienced major trauma in their journey to what they hoped would be a kinder place to live. Our children are often not safe.

Safety is also compromised by the growing climate emergency, and this generation of children is increasingly aware of how negligent the world has been in protecting the planet in favour of economic growth. As the evidence is writ large in heatwaves, fires, floods and storms, we cannot keep children away from these realities forever, although many try. Although their future Safety is insecure, we can support children's wellbeing by giving them Agency to take action and make changes in their own lives and surroundings where they can and learn to be global citizens (see chapter on Agency).

In school, we have the option to ensure children are safe to learn and thrive. Many educators are already making a significant difference to children's lives. It starts with the will to do this and the courage to follow through.

References, further reading and resources

Australian National Safe Schools Framework https://www.files.eric.ed.gov/fulltext/ED590680.pdf

Department for Education (2018 – updated 2022). *Working Together to Safeguard Children: Statutory Guidance (England)*.

Department for Education (2022). *Keeping Children Safe in Education: Statutory Guidance for schools and colleges*.

Gill, T. (2007). *No Fear: Growing Up in A Risk Averse Society*. Calouste Gulbenkian Foundation. This is now out of print, but a full copy can be downloaded at: https://www.timrgill.files.wordpress.com/2010/10/no-fear-19-12-07.pdf

Long, R., Robert, N. & Loft, P. (2020). *Bullying in UK Schools, Briefing Paper 8812*. House of Commons Library.

NAPCAN (n.d.). *Safer Communities for Children*. https://www.napcan.org.au/Programs/safer-communities-for-children/

Other sources and further reading

Bee, J. (2022). Wellbeing and Safeguarding. In K. Evans, T. Hoyle, F. Roberts & B. Yusuf (Eds.), *The Big Book of Whole School Wellbeing*. Corwin.

Booren, L.M., Handy, D.J. & Power, T.G. (2011). Examining Perceptions of School Safety Strategies, School Climate, and Violence. *Youth Violence and Juvenile Justice*, 9(2), 171–187.

Resources

The value of transitional objects for young children: https://www.babysparks.com/2019/10/08/
    transitional-objects-how-your-childs-favorite-stuffed-animal-promotes-social-emotional-
    development/
Australian National Safe Schools Framework https://www.files.eric.ed.gov/fulltext/ED590680.pdf
Mighty Heroes: https://www.esafety.gov.au/educators/classroom-resources/mighty-heroes
https://www.napcan.org.au/Programs/safer-communities-for-children/
Be an upstander – not a bystander. Prevent bullying: Four minute video: https://www.youtube.
    com/watch?v=eeqQCyQOCPg
https://www.raisingchildren.net.au/school-age/behaviour/bullying/school-bullying-helping
https://www.anti-bullyingalliance.org.uk/

3 Positivity
Strengths, solutions, smiles and support

What do we mean by Positivity?

In some ways Positivity has had a bad name. It is sometimes associated with a denial of the difficulties in life and a Pollyanna view in which everything has a rosy tinge. But Positivity in its many and varied facets has immense benefits for both individual and whole school wellbeing. It addresses and builds the following:

- Emotional wellbeing
- Self-construct and self-belief
- Values of kindness, consideration and support
- Strengths-based communication.
- Positive cognition and mindsets
- Meaningful and uplifting experiences
- Healthy relationships
- Constructive approaches to challenges
- A sense of fun and shared enjoyment.

The default position for many is the negative. People do not always seek to identify what is going well and how to get more of this and opt instead to spend time identifying deficits and dissecting what is wrong. They focus on why things don't work and how to fix them – usually as quickly and as cheaply as possible – often with short-term, unsustainable outcomes. Positivity costs nothing except the belief that it matters and the willingness to enact it. It may take more thought, but not necessarily more time or effort, than other ways of being, but it is undoubtedly more effective in promoting both learning and wellbeing.

This chapter explores how we can build Positivity throughout a school so that both pupils and teachers feel good about being there, the language used is supportive, there is a focus on building healthy relationships – including courtesy and kindness, and instead of taking problems apart, there are solution focused ways of coping with challenges.

Why does Positivity matter?

Congruence with the United Nations Convention on the Rights of the Child

Article 31 (leisure, play and culture): Every child has the right to relax, play and take part in a wide range of cultural and artistic activities.

Some children may not have positive feelings about themselves, others, or the world they are living in. Nothing much happens to them that gives them a sense of warmth, wonder or pride. They may hear negative talk much of the time, some of it about themselves. This leads

DOI: 10.4324/9781003428237-4

to a poor sense of self, and their behaviour and learning often reflect this. There are many reasons why it makes sense to build the positive in schools.

Positive child development

Children are precious – every one of them should know they are loved, valued and appreciated by those who spend time with them every day. They also are entitled to a childhood that is enriching and, as far as possible, joyful. Sometimes we seem to have forgotten what all children need for an optimal childhood experience that enables them to grow into the best they can be. Positivity in school has the potential to balance the hard situations that children may be experiencing outside.

Mental health and wellbeing

Deteriorating mental health for children and young people worldwide was the case before the pandemic and has worsened since. Although poverty increases family stress and impacts on positive functioning, economic circumstances are not the only reason children are not doing well. Adverse childhood experiences (ACEs) are clearly a prime cause, but other environmental factors are also involved. With early years and primary-aged children, these include anxiety about performance in school; worrying about what is happening at home; not being 'good enough', often fuelled by social media; bullying and social factors; and negative, neglectful or inconsistent parenting. Mental health concerns increase as children get older, but there are estimates that about three pupils in every primary classroom will have a diagnosable difficulty, with many others struggling from time to time but not reaching criteria for individual intervention. Not only do we need to consider the needs of all vulnerable children in education but also how to promote wellbeing for all. No one is exempt from issues that inhibit flourishing, including overprotection.

Healthy relationships

The quality of our relationships is at the crux of our happiness or misery. In schools these comprise peer relationships for both teachers and children, teacher-pupil, staff-executive and parent-school. Although healthy relationships require activation of all the ASPIRE principles, we focus here on Positivity. This includes a ratio of five positive interactions for every negative one. These micro-moments of high-quality interactions build expectations and relationships over time that enhance trust, support and collaboration. Although it is inevitable that at times we need to critique someone's behaviour, attitude or work, if we are also regularly noticing and commenting on their strengths, thanking them for their contributions and showing belief in the best of them, it is easier for that individual to listen to and accept criticism. They are less likely to be devastated by a negative comment if their sense of self has been fortified and they do not feel vulnerable.

Relationships are actioned by what is said and not said, and messages that are given about how we value someone. This includes interest, kindness, gratitude, generosity, respect and courtesy.

Positive thinking

Inner discourse

How we think about ourselves, other people, and situations that happen to us can either be predominantly negative or mostly positive. A pessimistic outlook is sometimes thought of as more realistic, but it can also lead to self-fulfilling expectations that can be harmful. Optimism, on the other hand, has links to better physical health, including longevity, coping skills, creativity, constructive problem-solving and positive social interactions. Children often have a strong preference for a particular way of thinking by the time they leave primary school – raising awareness of this and supporting a positive mindset is worthwhile.

Solution-focused

Rather than beginning with a problem, solution-focused thinking begins with what you want to achieve. When you have a vision of what a situation would look like with the difficulties resolved, you are then able to consider steps towards that goal. You identify what is already in place, what has worked well in the past, and what resources, skills and strategies you have at your disposal. You might then identify what else you might need and how others might help. This is often used for individuals in therapy but is also applicable to organisations such as schools. When school leaders identify a clear vision for their school, they can be more confident of the policies and processes developed to action this. It is OK to begin with the ideal even if you never get there – you at least know where you are heading.

Growth mindset

A fixed mindset is where someone believes they either have innate ability or they don't. A growth mindset is acknowledging that effort, persistence, good strategies and support can make all the difference to achievement. When children are told they are 'clever' or 'good at maths', they will be devastated when they do not do well, as this undermines who they believe they are. They may also blame others rather than evaluate their own efforts. A growth mindset is promoted by encouraging children to see that the more resources put into something, the more successful this will be. Carol Dweck (2017) has updated her views on growth mindset to say that it is not only effort that matters but a wide range of strategies to unlock learning.

Constructive problem-solving

One of the factors that underpin resilience is the positioning of difficulties as challenges rather than overwhelming obstacles. There are always options in any given situation, including doing nothing. Constructive problem-solving is a skill that can be taught. It includes brainstorming all possible options in response to a challenge and then reflecting on the pros and cons of each, including both inner and outer resources available. The penultimate stage is choosing one to try and another as back up with a review in a given time of how this is going. Constructive problem-solving not only engages creativity and courage but also reduces the power of negative emotions, especially feelings of helplessness.

Strengths-based approaches

The words that children hear about themselves influence their self-concept, especially if the people using them are significant in their lives – parents, extended family, carers and teachers. If we regularly tell children they are lazy, selfish or naughty, that is how they begin to think of themselves and live up to these expectations. Helping children identify their strengths – not just abilities – is a powerful antidote to this. Although Seligman's VIA strengths (Petersen & Seligman, 2004) are now used widely, there are many more expressed in simple language that are meaningful to children and young people. Here is an alternative framework that might be useful with primary-aged pupils (Roffey, 2011; Table 3.1). You can, of course, add more.

Table 3.1 Strengths

Interpersonal Strengths	Resilience Strengths	Ethical Strengths	Personal Strengths	Other Strengths
friendly	thankful	responsible	creative	sporting
willing to share	optimistic	honest	adventurous	musical
warm	keeps things in perspective	trustworthy	hard-working	artistic
caring	determined	fair	neat and tidy	imaginative
good listener	cheerful	acknowledges mistakes	sense of humour	graceful
helpful	sets goals	can make amends	energetic	good with animals
supportive	adaptable	respects confidentiality	enthusiastic	relaxed
fun to be with	inclusive	reliable	thoughtful	can fix things
considerate	can change	democratic	confident	colourful
interested	positive	asks questions	courageous	independent
kind	assertive	forgiving	careful	team player
empathic	problem solver	non-judgmental	curious	organised

Positive emotions

Negative emotions are diverse and have numerous expressions. Emotions such as anger, fear and disgust have a protective role in reacting rapidly to threat: a combination of emotional memory and circumstance combine to trigger the amygdala – the organ in the limbic system of the brain – leading to responses of fight, flight or freeze: run away fast, attack or pretend you're not there. It is usually when students perceive a threat – usually to their sense of self – that they react in ways that can be hard to manage. Note that it is the perception of threat that matters, not whether it consists of real danger or not. Unsurprisingly, it has been negative emotions that have been the focus of research.

The role of positive emotions has only comparatively recently received attention in psychological research. Although there are many and varied ways of feeling positive, they do not have the wide variety of expression that negative emotions do, because they do not activate responses in the same way. Some researchers have made a distinction between the definition of emotions and the definition of feelings. Emotions are embodied responses to stimuli, experienced physiologically, whereas feelings are subjective responses to how someone might interpret what is happening. We will, however, use the terms interchangeably here.

Positive psychology has made explicit what most teachers have known forever, that when children are full of anxiety, depression and fear, they do not function so well in the classroom, while positive feelings open up cognitive pathways and promote both creativity and problem-solving abilities. Fredrickson's 'broaden and build theory' (2001, 2013) suggests that positive emotions help us stay focused and expand our thinking, offering more options and strategies. They also undo the cardiovascular effects of negative emotions. Both support coping skills in the face of adversity. Positive feelings include feeling well, being interested, being comfortable, having fun, feeling pride, being connected with others, having hope and optimism and feeling acknowledged and valued. Play is one way to enhance positive emotions.

Play

Play is often positioned as a non-serious recreational activity, but it is much more than that for both wellbeing and learning. It is never aimless, even though the purpose might not be clear.

For all mammals, play is an important developmental activity. Young animals in their natural settings spend much of their early lives at play in order to learn strategies for survival. It might look like rough and tumble, but what the animals learn in these interactions informs them about what is and is not dangerous in their environment and how to react.

Children learn and grow through play. Play builds healthy brains, strengthens and extends physical development and enhances relationships, helping children to flourish across all domains of development. Play demands self-regulation, flexible thinking/problem-solving and memory. These core executive function skills underpin academic learning.

Play-based learning is, of course, not new. Based on her experiences of successfully teaching children living in slums in Rome, Maria Montessori developed a theory she called 'conductive learning'. This involves purposefully creating a classroom environment where each child plays/works at their own pace to master skills and concepts as they are ready. The role of early years professionals is to provide a wide range of materials, some of which are specifically designed, and encourage children to play, explore and interact with these. Adults observe, monitor and guide children's learning to promote curiosity and help them become independent and confident. They record progress in various curriculum areas so they can present children with appropriate activities to move them onto the next level, informing parents how to support this learning at home. New skills are honed through repetition until the child achieves mastery.

Play-based education underpins healthy development in several domains. The physical movement in play supports fitness and is usually enjoyable. It is also valuable in addressing the growing problem of obesity in today's young people. Collaborative play promotes more positive social interactions and is inherently creative, building flexible and innovative cognitive skills. It also helps children understand the need for agreed rules without which one person would dominate and the game would not work for everyone.

Make-believe, also known as imaginative or pretend play, is where children use props to develop their own scenarios and adventures, usually with others. This contributes to creative and innovative thinking, sometimes reliving situations and perhaps testing out different scenarios where the child takes charge.

Play scenarios have now gone online, and although there are benefits in developing some thinking and planning skills, they do not address equally important issues in other domains of development, social, physical and emotional.

Free play and mental health

Play is not just important for early years. Free play and exploration are how all children learn to solve problems, discover and develop interests, have autonomy and control away from adults and build a wide range of competencies. It is of concern that children's freedom to play has declined greatly in recent decades. Children no longer play with other kids down safe streets or go off on their bikes to the country or the beach before they are well into their teenage years. Adult-directed and monitored activities for children have increased, with more time in school than ever before, and the greatest significance given to success in academic subjects. Activities outside of school are also largely directed and controlled by adults.

Peter Gray (2011) researched the impact of reducing free play on the mental health of children and found a correlation between the decline of play and the rise in mental ill health amongst children and young people. Play builds resilience, helps traumatised children to adapt and cope and decreases stress. Learning through challenges that play presents is fun, rewarding and has no negative effects. Adventure playgrounds are useful, but only if parents let their children use them to the full and accept that they will choose diverse play companions.

When children are playing freely, making their own choices either alone or with others, they are interacting with the environment on their own terms, exploring and discovering with all their senses. With no adult-directed agenda, children can be creative, inventive, imaginative and self-reliant. This builds understanding, stimulates questions and promotes cognitive development generally. A child's positive sense of themselves is enhanced when they find themselves coping with the challenges presented by play. When children are interacting with others, this can build social competence and confidence, including appreciation of rules and boundaries, problem-solving and conflict resolution. Children may learn to manage aggression and bossiness when they find that this discourages others from playing with them.

Children may say they are bored if they are not offered activities on a plate and look to adults to provide entertainment. Boredom, however, can be the stimulus to discover what they can do for themselves. Unfortunately, many may resort to passive entertainment on screens rather than active engagement with the environment. Limiting screen time is a discussion many adults are now having.

Playfulness

Play is not the same as playfulness: in educational settings, playfulness boosts both positive behaviour and engagement in learning. This is a light-hearted way of injecting humour, warmth, connection and a sense of fun into the classroom – fostering the positive emotions that enhance learning and the sense of belonging that is a pillar of resilience and wellbeing. It is an approach to building a specific classroom culture. Humour is protective. People who can see the funny side of life's mishaps are likely to interpret and react to stress more positively, buffering themselves against some of the negative effects. Laughing releases oxytocin, thought to make us less likely to ruminate on or re-experience stressful events. It also helps to build relationships, providing the social support that is a key to resilience. It promotes connection, warmth, trust and collaboration. This in turn fosters resilience.

Behaviour

There is a Cherokee story about the two wolves who exist inside a person and battle for their spirit – one tries to live in harmony with those around them and do no harm, not jumping to judgment about the intention of others, while the other wolf is full of anger and will fight for no reason. A child asks his grandfather which wolf wins, and the grandfather says, "The one that you feed".

The more attention you give to unwanted behaviour, the more it will dominate. It is better to focus on, acknowledge and build behaviours that promote the positive. This means talking about what is expected, having clear routines that children can follow, giving reminders rather than reprimands when children forget and regularly thanking pupils for being helpful, kind, thoughtful or making an effort.

- "I like the way you ..."
- "I have noticed that ..."
- "I wonder if ..." (can be a gentle suggestion for taking the positive one step further)
- "Well done for..."

Asking children what they feel when they have achieved something, especially if it has been complex or difficult, or demonstrated a strength, will help them realise that some ways of being are more likely to make them feel good about themselves.

This is particularly important for those children who come to school full of negative feelings about themselves and the world generally. They may be disruptive or not compliant with direction because they fear failure or have a poor sense of self. They may be aggressive because they have learnt to expect rejection.

This does not mean that unacceptable behaviour is ignored. A conversation that shows children you have belief in the best of them, and asks how they are going to repair the damage they have caused, gives them a second chance. It is also worth having solution-focused conversations. "What did you want to happen?" "What might have been a better way of getting there?" Giving pupils a reason to feel worse about themselves than they already do is likely to backfire.

See the section on restorative approaches in the chapter on Inclusion.

Putting Positivity in practice in the early years

Early years teachers are skilled at offering opportunities to young children that encourage them to explore, ask questions and experiment. This stimulates their interest in the world around them and is the basis of internal motivation – learning because they love it.

Communication

What happens in children's first days and weeks in an educational setting, whether this is an early years provision or primary school, influences how an individual sees themselves as a learner. How the adults respond to their efforts and interactions can either give them a positive and optimistic view of learning or the impression that trying things out is scary, as it may meet with disapproval or that they are no good at this.

Strengths-based language reinforces both a growth mindset and a positive self-concept. Encouragement to have another go, giving commendation for trying, and letting children know when they have achieved a small step in the right direction, all help. Using the word 'yet' indicates that this is something they will learn or have eventually, and promotes optimism, effort and perhaps patience! There is a gaping difference between "you can't do that", and "you are not able to do that yet, but you are getting there".

Communication with the parents and carers is also critically important. Messages home about a child's strengths, achievements and efforts are not only valuable for the child in reinforcing motivation, but also for the parents in helping them see themselves as valued and competent adults. Some early years educators take photos and/or videos of children participating in various activities so that parents can see the wide variety of learning opportunities offered to their children and be reassured that they are in good hands. This also gives topics for following up at home, both in conversation and activities.

This is an example of a brief positive letter home about a two-year-old that covers aspects of their personality, learning, interests, social inclusion and the impact she has on others.

Young Friends Kindergarten: Brighton

Maya has started nursery with such confidence and laughter. Maya is friendly and likes to include everyone in her games. Her favourite areas at nursery are the home corner, garden and art room in which she loves to explore her favourite topics such as insects, mark making, rainbows, home life and cooking. Cooking is a particular passion of Maya's and is she always eager to cook. Her cooking skills have really progressed in such a short time and she has an emerging awareness that meals involve a variety of different ingredients, that need to be grown and harvested not simply bought from a store. Recently Maya took the younger children on a walk about the garden to "strawberry pick" to add to her "pancakes".

Maya is such a lively presence and brightens our day each time she's in.

For parents who might be struggling, words such as these may have a powerful influence on how they position both their child and themselves. It is informative, reassuring, motivating and helpful. It is also on paper rather than text so it can be kept and perhaps shown to others, sharing and reinforcing the positive. If difficulties do emerge, the family will be much more willing to listen to concerns that staff express and be involved in discussing what might be done, because the staff have already shown that they see the child positively and have their best interests at heart. Compare this to a letter home that lists a child's misdemeanours and the problems they are causing: parents will feel blamed, and either be angry and defensive or never be seen again. Words have far-reaching consequences.

Play

Imaginative play is a valuable feature of early years settings, and the 'dressing up box' can contain stimulus outfits from a full doctor's outfit to a range of different hats. Children try on different characters, make up scenarios and take control of situations. Playing hospital may help children re-experience a stressful visit and this time have more control of their feelings. They may be taking the part of a doctor or nurse, so also thinking about empathy. Pretending to be a mermaid or a horse can give free rein (!) to exploring emotions. Pre-schoolers also begin to realise that objects can be manipulated and be used for a variety of purposes. A blanket thrown over a table can become a cave, a cardboard box a boat and a tree a giant with perhaps a tiny village amongst the roots with children using flowers, blocks and other materials for imaginary houses, gardens and people to boost their stories. Books give children initial ideas, but with permission and time they can expand and develop these – building brains as they do. Giving children plenty of notice for the end of a play session matters, especially for those who find any transition hard. Being suddenly torn away mid-adventure might lead to frustration, fury and hard-to-manage behaviour!

Supporting positive behaviour

It is never too early to teach children the concept of 'gentle' and give them opportunities to practice this – holding and stroking animals, passing fragile items, treating baby brothers and sisters with care. Keeping pre-schoolers away from things that might break does not teach them how to look after fragile objects, and they are then more likely to be rough. If they are also told how gentle they are becoming, they will then see this as a strength and try to live up to it. If a child does damage something, telling them they are careless or clumsy will reinforce a negative self-concept. Accidents do happen, which is why we need to practice being gentle.

Unless children are tired, unwell or anxious, repetition on what is acceptable reinforces expectations and will eventually become part of routine. Giving information is more effective than reprimands:

- Crayons are for paper, not the floor.
- Balls are thrown outside.
- Please use your inside voice in here.

Children who have heard these statements several times can be asked to respond to questions to show they know what to do. Where do we use crayons? Is that your inside or outside voice? And so on.

No child should hear themselves described as 'naughty'. It is a word that rolls off the tongue in many situations, but it reinforces a negative sense of self – and perhaps a character trait – that is best avoided. Other children hear how their peers are described and treat them accordingly. Children need to live up to the positive they hear about themselves, not live down to the negative.

Emotional regulation

Emotional regulation can be hard for small children, but it is a skill that needs to begin early.

Helping them recognise how emotions are experienced in their bodies is a start. Even small children can learn about 'belly breathing', which helps anyone become calmer. There is an engaging *Sesame Street* clip that shows how this works (see Resources).

If they are not to use their fists and feet when frustrated, children need to learn words for feelings. It is not uncommon to hear adults in pre-school settings say to children, "Use your words". It is also helpful for children to learn to begin sentences with 'I' rather than 'you' in social situations such as, "I don't like that"; "I need space"; "I want to play with the bike". When resources are limited, children need to learn the skills of negotiation, sharing and taking turns. Talking with groups of children about what is fair before clashes occur can limit conflict (see Activities in SEL at the end of this chapter).

When they are upset, acknowledging what has happened and the feelings associated, and giving them permission to express these safely, can help to calm a situation more quickly. If the child has enough language, they can later be encouraged to talk about what happened and perhaps asked to think what they might do in a similar situation. Many people underestimate young children's ability to problem-solve when given the opportunity.

Putting Positivity in practice in the primary classroom

The NSW Commission for Children and Young People asked students to say what they thought characterised a good teacher. The responses included that a teacher tries to make learning fun, that they "smile at me" and "ask me how I'm doing but not just in school". The value of fun to support engagement in learning is worldwide. Here is an example from India.

SOS Children's Villages

One in 10 children and young people across the world are separated from their families; abandoned, neglected or caught up in disasters, SOS Children's Villages is an international organisation working in over 130 countries. They are dedicated to improving the lives of children and young people without parental care or at risk of losing it. This enables children to grow up with the bonds they need to develop and become their strongest selves. Children without kinship carers are placed in 'family' group homes in villages. The following is from a 2023 newsletter:

Fun and Learn at CV Jammu

There has been some notable growth in aspects of activities and academics in SOS Children's Village Jammu, India. Learning becomes easy when combined with fun. With audio and visual graphics available in the village, teaching young children about different topics is more accessible. Fun activities combined with learning help engage young children who may not enjoy studying.

Nisha says: "Playing the word and letter games with my friend and teacher is vibrant and exciting. I have learned many new words and meanings with pictures".

Sanjay says "I enjoy different sounds of alphabets through audio sessions"

(Names have been changed)

Teacher-student relationships

There is now a wealth of evidence confirming that the quality of the relationship between teacher and student makes a significant difference to learning outcomes. This includes getting to know something about each pupil at the beginning of the school year. Educators can then utilise this information to show interest and appreciation that builds positive relationships and the ability to more effectively support children's learning. This saves time later on picking up the pieces when things go awry.

Relationships are built in the thousands of micro-moments that take place in the classroom every day. Choosing the positive takes no more time and effort than defaulting to the negative. Here is an acronym that might help:

Going WALKIES

WELCOME pupils, look pleased to see them, using their name if you can remember it and asking them to remind you if you can't. Over time, perhaps find a positive word that is alliterative with their name (e.g. Joyful Joe, Marvellous Morgan, Splendid Sami, Kind Keira). Ask if they like this word or if they would like to choose a different one.

ACKNOWLEDGE their presence, efforts and achievements – not just in work but in character and strength development.

LISTENING is hard for busy teachers, but 20 seconds of full attention can enable a pupil to feel heard. Circle sessions give opportunities for every student to speak, even if briefly.

KINDNESS is not just in the things we do but in the words we say. Teacher wellbeing is essential so that words stay thoughtful and not knee-jerk responses to stressful situations.

INVITATION either to participate with others or just for their opinion, shows that someone matters.

ENTHUSIASM is a great gift for an educator – it works wonders in engaging students. But being enthusiastic about students themselves and their efforts – even going over the top to make everyone laugh – can also bring benefits.

SMILING is a universal and powerful indicator of friendliness and connection. Regularly smiling at students lifts everyone up and generates a culture of warmth across a class.

SILENCES – there are times when it is important to say something and times when words can make something worse. Much of the time a criticism is redundant – the person already knows they messed up; they don't need others to tell them.

Teaching and learning

Case study: Positive pedagogy

Mia O'Brien and Levon Blue (2018) carried out an action research project with teachers to explore Positivity in the primary classroom. The study took place over six school terms, initially with three classroom teachers but later with 14 teachers across all grades plus a language teacher. Data was collected from both teachers and students.

Teachers noted that many students did not initially demonstrate positive engagement in learning. They arrived in class unprepared, with high levels of anxiety and quickly gave up when faced with challenges. The first aim therefore was to create an explicitly positive and engaging classroom culture. The second was to build the personal, psychological and social resources that facilitate a positive experience of learning in classrooms.

Early discussions with the action research team led to the development of the PALS framework (Positive Agile Learners) which identified key learning-related behaviours that would support students in positively facing challenges. Presented on posters in every class, they included the following:

- Performing – paying attention, following directions, working with self-control, leading and helping others, staying motivated and completing tasks.
- Innovating – asking questions, finding different ways to do things, brainstorming and creating, overcoming roadblocks.
- Taking a risk – having a go, trying something even when you're unsure, experimenting, developing solutions.
- Reflecting – thinking about your own learning, learning from mistakes, looking at the big picture, remembering your 'best self'!
- Overcoming roadblocks – accepting feedback, being open and flexible, changing tactics and joining in, talking to the teacher.
- Students were introduced to the PALs posters and asked to consider who they were when they were being their 'best self'. At a later date they were also asked what got in the way of them being their 'best self'. Teachers linked the reminders in the PALs poster to units of work, and as lessons unfolded made use of the poster in various ways, developing strategies and engaging students in sharing their own ideas.

There were many discussions, amendments and sharing during the research cycle – contexts changed and practices evolved. But findings from both teachers and students identified useful classroom practices that facilitated positive pedagogies. These included:

- Having a positive language to use with children: e.g. *"How are you going to overcome this roadblock?"*
- Talking about how to learn and take risks with learning: *"I stayed motivated; I had a go"*.
- Children recognising mistakes as learning opportunities.
- Different more positive ways of relating with one another.

Outcomes included:

- More positive inner dialogue for teachers and recognising that changes in thinking affected activities in the classroom. Some said that it gave them a deeper emotional resonance with their values in becoming a teacher.
- Attitudes to learning became more positive: "*I felt encouraged to learn.*" "*I figured out how to read more tricky books.*"
- Improved behaviour: "*Before I didn't learn so much because I was always naughty, but having PALS helped me overcome roadblocks and not get angry – so I did lots more learning and didn't get into trouble nearly as much*".

Playfulness

Playfulness diffuses conflict and creates connection. A playful teacher sets the tone for a peaceful, positive-emotion fuelled classroom, moving beyond the need to rely on operant behaviour management systems or power dynamics.

(Tidmund, 2021)

Playfulness is creative, fun and sometimes just silly – which children love. It brings back the joy of being young into the educational setting. It also allows teachers to be in charge of proceedings without controlling pupils.

A light-hearted approach both engages children and reduces anxiety. Laughing together increases a sense of belonging. There are many ways to do this. Teachers can make fun of themselves to good effect. It is valuable when teachers own a mistake – sometimes a deliberate one – as it gives permission for pupils to also do this. The following strategy is one way of having a 'conversation' you want children to hear but is not directed at them. Puppets or soft toys can fulfil the same function – depending on the age of the pupils.

Pauli Pane:

Pauli Pane is a cut-out picture of a life-sized child taped onto the window of the classroom. This figure does not have to represent reality and can be roughly drawn, multi-coloured and gender neutral. The teacher has conversations with Pauli about what is happening in the classroom, expressing pleasure at how well an activity is going or the positive behaviour of children. "Just look, Pauli, at what these children have done this morning, I am so proud of them". The figure also presents an opportunity for the teacher to express concern at what is not happening. "Pauli, I wonder how long I am going to have to wait before everyone is quiet enough to hear me. I do think it's getting quieter. Yes, only one or two people talking now".

Pauli also gives teachers a way to express frustration and other negative emotions without directing this at real children, protecting the wellbeing of both!

Kindness

Kindness costs nothing, but not every child knows what it is, nor understands how it not only helps others, but can make themself feel good too. There are many activities to promote kindness across a class, but this is particularly effective – and fun:

Bucket filling:

Even young children can quickly understand the concept of 'bucket fillers' and 'bucket dippers'. The fillers are things that people do or say that make someone feel good; the dippers do the opposite.

Children first identify – perhaps in pairs – what makes a good friend. Going around in a circle, they then share this with everyone. These actions are written up as bucket fillers. They then think about themselves as bucket fillers – things they can do and say that are kind – not just to friends but to all children in their class, to others in the school, or for the environment. Pictures of buckets on the wall with phrases such as, "Say thanks for something"; "Pick up rubbish and put it in the bin"; ask, "How are you doing today?" or remind children of all the possibilities for kindness.

The question/reflection, "How did you fill someone's bucket today?", can be asked at the end of each day to keep the idea alive. Perhaps at the end of the week children can brainstorm what they might do next week as a class. There are many more ideas for extending bucket-filling ideas in the resources at the end of the chapter.

The value of a strengths approach

Adopting a strengths focus in schools can positively shape personal wellbeing, relationships and school culture. Human beings have a negativity bias that is hardwired to pay attention to threat and danger. This means we are good at noticing what's wrong but tend to overlook or not notice what's going right. We believe we see the full picture, but attention is more like a laser beam than a floodlight, so when we are fully focused on what's not working, we may miss seeing what is going well. In schools, that is a disadvantage for building positive relationships as well as for learning and problem-solving.

1 Knowing the negatives about someone tells you nothing about their positive qualities.
2 It's easier to feel connected to someone who notices what's good about you than with someone who only points out your flaws or errors.
3 The seeds of a solution to any problem lie in what's working, not in what's broken.

Adopting a strengths focus is an effective way of compensating for this ingrained negativity bias. It means learning to pay attention to the many ways things do go right and the positives that people bring to a situation. The simplest description of a strength is something you do well and enjoy. Because people enjoy using their strengths, it is helpful to watch out for the things that people are eager to do and energised by doing.

Every student and teacher needs to know their strengths so they can use and build on them. Individuals who know and use their strengths are 18 times more likely to have a higher level of wellbeing than those who don't. Strength awareness is also associated with greater engagement, self-efficacy and wellbeing. We feel better about ourselves when we focus on the things we do well and enjoy doing. This increased engagement and self-efficacy can unlock virtuous learning cycles.

Strengths Specs *(with thanks to Sybilla Gerden):*

This is a way to get children to identify strengths in each other and can be powerful in generating a strengths-based perspective across the whole class.

The teacher accesses a number of different spectacle frames – perhaps about ten. These are sometimes available in charity shops or from relatives who have new glasses and are pleased to find a purpose for the old ones. The more diverse and quirky the frames the better. The lenses are pushed out, they are not needed. Each different pair of specs is labelled, such as the kindness specs, good listening, sharing, gentleness, helpful, caring, good leadership, patience. You choose. They need to be strengths that can be demonstrated. The teacher identifies a student in a session who has shown a particular strength, and they wear the specs for the rest of that session until the next break. Their role is to look through the strength specs they are wearing to notice other students demonstrating the same strength. Although children will begin by choosing their own friends, this soon changes. The teacher ensures that over time all children get a chance to wear the specs – and children can perhaps choose the strengths they feel are important for their class.

Putting Positivity in practice across the primary school

When play is infused throughout the school ethos, there is a paradigm shift. Play generates positive emotions, which revitalise and renew individual and collective reserves for problem-solving and prosocial behaviour. It is mind-expanding, literally; embracing play widens attention spans, broadens frames of reference and promotes prosocial behaviour.

(Tidmund, 2021)

It is hard for teachers to be light-hearted and playful in an environment where they are under great pressure to deliver high academic outcomes. They may also have less tolerance for pupils who are not focused, compliant or achieving. It is not only sad but dangerous for our children's future when negativity dominates school culture. It is, however, not inevitable. There are many schools across the world meeting children's needs in a healthy, positive way that also supports everyone with their learning. This does not mean ignoring problematic issues, but ensuring that both students and teachers feel good about being there and that the culture is warm and supportive and as far as possible, learning is joyful.

A teacher once told me that, although they were obliged to carry out the national tests that everyone was mandated to do, the senior leadership team at her school were determined they would not be the focus of conversation or classroom practice for weeks beforehand. This showed staff they had confidence in their teaching. The tests came and went, and results were on a par with others. Wellbeing was the priority and anxiety kept at a minimum.

It is not only the children, however, who benefit from playfulness. When this is promoted across an organisation it also boosts the wellbeing of adults. Experiencing positive emotions has the same outcomes as with children for engagement and learning. With individuals it can also enhance motivation and meaning. Playfulness with others can generate aspects of positive relationships, such as trust and collaboration.

Playtimes

As we have seen, play is vital for children's physical, mental and social well-being. Playtime is therefore an important part of the day for all children, and needs to be protected. Evidence shows that even a small increase in playtime can improve children's emotional wellbeing (Burson & Castelli, 2022). To optimise children's experience, however, this needs to be taken seriously, planned for, actioned with thought, and regularly reviewed. This will include consideration of the outside space in the school, how this is used and what changes might be made to make playtime better for everyone. Playground policy will also address the accessibility of different activities for pupils with diverse needs and the role of playground supervisors.

Positive Playtimes: Thérèse Hoyle

I work with primary schools internationally developing active and engaging playtimes. In our initial audit with a school, we frequently find that children are bored at playtimes, there's not much for them to do, and sometimes the only resource available is a football!

Equal opportunities for all children mean thinking through the play space available, offering a mixture of free play and more structured activities and ensuring every child's needs are met.

Years ago, when teaching in New Zealand, a parent once told me how worried she was about her son at playtimes. He had started to think there was something wrong with him because he didn't want to play sport and that was all there was to do. She said he'd just like to read or play a board game.

So, we created a quiet area, which he loved and today in our schools we have Quiet Zones where children can sit and colour, read books or play board games. A zone for more active children is the Craze Area where a new activity is introduced each week. Having different equipment gives children a sense of purpose where they get to build relationships, learn new skills, different moves or rhymes with skipping ropes, hoola-hoops or balls. Parachute games and space hopper challenges are also great fun! Creative children like to sing and dance in the performance zone or dress up in the imaginative play zone. Here they can play with a tea set, make a den out of loose parts, investigate wildlife with a magnifying glass or make towers out of plastic crates!

The diversity of play opportunities increases wellbeing, improves behaviour and develops positive relationships. After six months of taking part in our Positive Playtime Masterclass Programme, Oasis Ryelands in Croydon have seen a 70% decrease in aggressive behaviour at playtimes with arguments and fights now rare. Children commented how much they love the range of equipment and activities, with a new craze activity each week and staff teaching and playing games in the playground such as Tic Tac Toe Relay and the more traditional such as What's the Time Mr Wolf? One said: "I know the adults care, because they play games with us".

Thérèse Hoyle: Founder of the Positive Playtime Program, and author of 101 Playground Games and 101 Wet Playtime Games. https://www.theresehoyle.com

Strengths across a school

A strengths approach goes beyond the benefits to individuals – it has much wider benefits in that it builds relationships and transforms group culture. Strengths spotting is the name commonly given to the practice of noticing and commenting on strengths in others. It is the practice that unlocks the relational power of the strengths approach. When teachers focus on noticing what's going well with students, situations and their own teaching, this has the potential to transform the culture in which they work and learn.

The power of a strengths approach for building a positive school culture

The research I conducted with students and their teachers in primary and intermediate schools in New Zealand demonstrated the relational and cultural power of the strengths approach. Through a classroom-based programme, students learned about their strengths and were encouraged to notice strengths in others. They practiced strengths spotting in class, peer to peer, and teachers were encouraged to notice strengths in students.

These practices improved student wellbeing, behavioural and emotional engagement in the classroom, improved connectedness between students. They improved class social climate through increased cohesion and less friction. Several teachers independently reported that there was less teasing and bullying in their classrooms. One teacher noted that students were not only were more accepting of each other, they were now protective of their classmates in the wider school playground.

Results from this study also demonstrated the powerful role that teachers play in influencing classroom behaviour. The positive outcomes were directly driven (mediated in statistical terms) by teacher behaviour. Where teachers reported higher levels of strengths spotting in their students, students reported greater benefits from the programme. This finding suggests that the role of teachers in strengths programmes is pivotal for their success. Where teachers are supportive of and engage with strengths practices, including role modelling and strengths spotting, students are more likely to adopt these practices, including in peer-to-peer relationships.

Dr Denise Quinlan: Director, New Zealand Institute of Resilience and Wellbeing

Staff wellbeing

If we want our children to be nurtured, we must cherish our teachers. In countries such as Finland, teachers are held in high regard, given professional autonomy, and paid well. There is strong competition to enter the profession, with about one in ten applicants being successful. Higher teacher wellbeing is associated with effectiveness and improved student outcomes, retention, resilience and job satisfaction. Teacher retention is a concern in many countries as stress and burnout take their toll, with experienced educators leaving the profession and possible recruits lacking the motivation to join. Research indicates that in the UK teachers consider their wellbeing lower than most other professions, including health, social work, finance and human resources (Grenville-Cleave & Boniwell, 2012). Teacher mental health is undermined by increased demands for accountability, frequent innovations, an inflexible imposed curriculum, a high workload, and insufficient time to establish the relationships with pupils that bring the greatest satisfaction to the role. Staff absence leads to inconsistent and fragmented teaching, and this in turn impacts on both wellbeing and learning for students. It makes sense for every school to promote teacher wellbeing as an essential feature of whole-school wellbeing.

Staff wellbeing is a multi-dimensional construct that incorporates personal approaches and systemic interventions. Interestingly, levels of burnout do not seem to be related to school context, as teachers may be doing well in areas of disadvantage where their job is highly challenging, and choosing to leave more privileged schools whose culture is toxic. What matters is what is going on in schools to support staff. Teachers are often asked to 'look after' their own wellbeing by actions such as taking exercise, getting enough sleep and finding time to relax with friends and family, but that will be insufficient if organisational expectations and processes are not aligned. Here is a summary of the positive school factors associated with higher teacher wellbeing:

- A supportive and positive school climate and school leaders who generate this
- Caring social relationships and collaboration where teachers support each other and work together
- Shared vision and values
- A professional setting that encourages quality teaching

- Support for autonomy
- Positive teacher-student relationships that provide meaning
- Support from mentors which is of particular relevance for early career teachers
- Basic structures such as good staffroom facilities, sufficient break times, scheduling only necessary meetings, and clear expectations for when staff are available and not.

Workload

No one can do everything to a high standard of excellence and stay mentally well. The pressure is too great. This applies to both teachers and pupils. School leaders need to work with staff to decide priorities and what can be completed to a level that is acceptable but not consistently 'outstanding'. It is the difference between writing a page of useful and relevant bullet points in a report and writing four pages of prose that takes most of a weekend.

Activity: Secret angels:

Every member of staff who wants to be involved in this initiative puts their name in a hat at the beginning of term. They then take out the name of someone else. The first person is the secret angel for the second. Their role is to check in with them from time to time, make them the occasional tea or coffee, put a card or cookie in their pigeonhole, perhaps take a playground duty for them or celebrate their birthday if they have one during the term. It doesn't take long to discover your secret angel! The important thing is that teachers have each other's backs and are there for each other when times are tough.

Positive thinking

Optimism

Optimistic thinking is where someone anticipates positive outcomes but also has cognitive strategies that stop them being overwhelmed when things do not go to plan. It is the opposite of the learned helplessness that Martin Seligman says is at the root of depression. He has written about both (Petersen, Maier & Seligman, 1995; Seligman, 2006). Optimism is hope for the future, and can be encouraged in school by the conversations that take place. As mentioned earlier, the word 'yet' is particularly valuable, as it shows that learning is on a trajectory, and that there is still some way to go. Optimistic thinking may require some reframing of a situation to avoid catastrophising. Normalising a difficult event, such as breaking something, helps children put things into perspective, e.g., "These things happen sometimes; let's just clear up the mess". Adults showing children how to do this is an effective teaching strategy. Sometimes this means admitting you were wrong or modelling a response that affirms that making an error isn't the end of the world. Being able to laugh at yourself illustrates that imperfection is human and OK.

Gratitude

When gratitude permeates school culture, it generates multiple positive outcomes. It can be defined in three ways – a feeling of thankfulness, an appreciative thought and acknowledgement in action. Here we focus on the little things that schools might do to build positive relationships by showing gratitude. In some places this is harder than others as, like most things, gratitude is driven by context. But modelling gratitude alongside other positive ways of being can be contagious. The more it happens, the more likely it will become embedded.

With pupils

- All staff are encouraged to recognise any effort that students have made. For some, just getting to school in the morning is an achievement.
- Over time, ask pupils to find out about the roles of different people who work in the school, such as the cleaner, the caretaker and the school admin staff. What do they do, when do they do it, what difference does this make to how the school runs? They then write thank-you notes, perhaps making the letters specific for things that matter most to them. In one school, a class left a bunch of flowers or a bar of chocolate for the cleaner from time to time. Their classroom was especially sparkly!
- At home-time, make it a policy to ask pupils to think of one thing they learnt that day they found interesting or enjoyed knowing about and share this with a partner or the teacher as they leave the classroom.

With families

- Position families as experts on their child and thank them for sharing this knowledge with you.
- Thank people for coming to meetings, especially parents for whom it might be a struggle.
- Both in writing reports and in meetings begin with the positive about the child. Say what they have achieved, the strengths they have demonstrated and something about them that you value/like. This does several things. It shows you have the child's best interests at heart. It promotes positive and trusting relationships, and it means that if you have something difficult to discuss later on, families will be more willing to listen.

With staff

- Putting affirmations in staff pigeonholes can lift their day and make them feel appreciated. This is not necessarily about good work but about the personal qualities they bring to the job.
- In whole school Circle Solutions training, I have sometimes asked everyone to tape a piece of paper on their back and then all staff to write on the paper what they value about them as a colleague, usually limiting this to ten statements, each numbered. The last person takes the paper, folds it into four and gives it to their colleague. The activity only ends when everyone has the requisite ten statements. Staff are then asked to sit back in the Circle, open their paper all together and read what has been said about them. They are asked to reflect on the following:

  - What this makes them feel about themselves and the day they are having
  - What this makes them feel about the colleagues they work with who have written positive things
  - What this makes them understand about some of the pupils they teach.

- Some teachers have said that this brief activity changed how they felt about teaching in the school, and they gained valuable insight about their relationships with both colleagues and pupils.

Other staff

- We need to take care of all those who work in schools, including non-teaching staff.
- Some schools have introduced a Random Act of Kindness Board. This is where individuals can put up Post-it notes to thank someone for going out of their way to inform, share, offer, support or simply show empathy for someone having a hard time. It applies to everyone in the school and is cleared on a regular basis, so there are opportunities for new starts.

Case study

The principal of a school in NSW sent out a newsletter every Friday. On the front page was a thank you to someone in the school – perhaps a teacher, parent, non-teaching staff or community member. This was not just for special events and achievements but for everyday good work. Staff said that this was the first thing everyone was interested in – who was being acknowledged this week.

Positivity in social and emotional learning (SEL)

One of the main reasons Circle Solutions works well, and children regularly ask for it, is that they have fun. Many of the activities in Circles are presented as games, and some of these have no other purpose than to generate laughing together. Children who have a good time together in Circles are more likely to be friendly and supportive outside the Circle. Some also learn that having fun does not have to be at the expense of others.

Positivity is also demonstrated by focusing on solutions rather than problems. Circles are the place to identify strengths for each other and for the whole class.

Activities in SEL

Strengths

Strengths in Circles Cards:

There are seven statements for each of the six ASPIRE principles.
These are three of those for Positivity:

* We laugh together.
* We celebrate together.
* We want the best for each other.

In groups of three or four students, take one statement at a time and discuss the following questions together:

– What does this mean?
– Is this what we want in our class?
– What would it make people feel about being here?
– Is it already happening – how do we know?
– What else might we do?
– What help might we need?

Each group decides on one action. They give a brief report back to the Circle, emphasising the action. What they all agree is put on display as a reminder.

Strengths identification:

Play a game that mixes pupils up so that they are sitting next to someone who is not necessarily a friend. Spread strength cards or photos in the centre of the Circle. Ask each person to pick up a card that represents a strength that they have noticed in their partner and then tell each other why they have chosen this.

Star of the Circle:

Pupils each have a turn to be the Star. Everyone knows who it will be next time so they can look out for and report on the positive. This pupil leaves the Circle, and the teacher goes around asking everyone to contribute to the statement about their strengths and contributions. This is written down, and when the student comes back into the Circle, the teacher reads out what everyone has said. It is then given to that pupil to take home and keep.

Mindfulness

Mindfulness is focusing on the present moment, the bodily sensations you are experiencing, and being objective about thoughts and feelings. Although the evidence for the benefits of mindfulness in primary education is not strong, it is worth including aspects of this in closing Circle activities to promote calmness and attention skills. It can be combined with relaxation activities. Doing this regularly will help children understand the value of being in the moment. This can relieve anxiety.

Squeeze and release:

Ask children to sit comfortably with their feet on the floor and close their eyes. Ask them to tighten and squeeze the muscles in their feet and then release them, now in their legs and then their bottom. Go on up the body, including hands and arms and ending with screwing up their face. At the end, you can ask children to stand up, stretch up as high as they can and then flop forward.

Glitter bottles:

Show children a bottle full of water. Add a big spoonful of glitter, put a lid on and shake it up. Tell them that this is what it is like when they are full up with lots of feelings. It is hard to think clearly. The children watch while the glitter slowly falls to the bottom of the bottle and point out that as this happens, they can see the water clearly.

Ask them to close their eyes and think about all the feelings that they might have and imagine them settling down to the bottom of their mind so they don't get in the way.

Inside and out listening:

Ask children to sit comfortably with their feet on the floor and close their eyes. Here is a script teachers can follow:

We need to be very quiet, because we are going to be listening to all the different sounds we can hear.
First of all, listen to your breathing going in and out - perhaps breathe in through your nose and out through your mouth – in and out.
You might be able to hear your heart beating – perhaps you can feel that rather than hear it.
Perhaps your tummy is rumbling!
Now listen to all the sounds inside our classroom – is there a squeak anywhere?

Now, what you can hear outside – traffic, people talking, birds singing, dogs barking.
Take a deep breath again, open your eyes and talk to the person next to you about all the
things you heard. Did you hear the same sounds? I will partner with (name a pupil on
one side of you), so now go round the Circle pairing up.

Positive thinking skills

BLESSINGS

There is now much evidence to confirm that having a positive mindset that focuses on what is going well rather than mistakes, imperfections and disasters is a powerful factor for resilience and wellbeing. It makes sense to boost this thankfulness mentality where possible, making children aware of what they do have. It also helps in reducing a sense of entitlement and promotes empathy for those who have fallen on hard times.

Count your Blessings:

Everyone wanders around in the middle of the Circle and at a given signal partners with the person nearest to them – or forms a group of three. The first time, they have a conversation about what they are thankful for this week – anything that has gone well. Ensure there is enough time for all pupils to speak if they wish. They then mix up again, and at a second signal they find a new partner or group. This time, they talk about something they have been pleased about this year. Finally, after mixing up again, they talk with a new partner or group about something that they are grateful for in their life generally, such as being able to listen to music or having a pet.

The Wellbeing Stories:

These stories use a narrative approach by representing positive and negative thinking as fictional characters – such as the Worry Wart, the If-Only Elf, Common Sense and the Organisational Owl – in six stories. There are ten short chapters in each story and Circle Solutions activities in the Teacher Toolkits for each chapter.

In William and the Worry Wart there is an activity that introduces Common Sense, the character who sticks to the facts rather than letting negative imagination go into overdrive. Students work in pairs to decide whether these statements are more likely to be said by a Worry Wart voice or a Common Sense voice when someone is faced with an upcoming test:

Statement	Worry Wart	Common Sense
My mind will go blank		
I must remember to read the question carefully		
They will ask me something I don't know		
Everyone will think I am a loser		
Most of my friends will be feeling the same as me		
I will just do my best		

They can now make up another statement for each voice and share it with the Circle.

LAUGHING GAMES

Remember to remind pupils they can choose to 'pass' if they prefer to just watch.

Find your furry friends:

Have the names of six animals – cow, dog, cat, sheep, pig and bee. Each pupil has the name of one. Check that they all know what sound each makes. Ask pupils to get down on the ground and find their friends with sound alone. If you have a smaller class, you need fewer animals!

Finding not very furry friends:

Have the names of these six animals – penguin, elephant, rabbit, eagle, jellyfish and shark. (Or kangaroo, bear, dolphin, snake, mouse and giraffe). Ask students to show you how each of these creatures would move. Go round the Circle giving each pupil the name of one of these – this can be whispered or written down on a piece of card. At a given signal, they move around to find their not-very-furry friends moving as if they were that creature without making a sound.

Crocodiles:

First, play a game to mix everyone up, and then each pupil partners with the person sitting next to them. Give each pair a piece of newspaper and ask them to stand on it. This is their safe 'island' in a river full of crocodiles. Now they pick up their island and walk around the Circle until the teacher calls out 'Crocodile', and they all stand on their 'island' for a count of five. They then fold the paper in half so that they are standing on a smaller 'island'. The game goes on with folding the paper in half every time and counting to five. When someone falls off their 'island', they are out and sit back in the Circle. Children will think of all sorts of ways to try and balance but will often fall off because they are laughing so hard!

Positivity checklist

POSITIVITY	This is in place – we know it is effective because ...	Working on it – our actions to date are ...	Just started – our next step will be ...
Strengths-based approach			
A range of play opportunities			
Solution-focused conversations			
Focus on teacher wellbeing			
Positive actions – kindness, gratitude, playfulness			
Positive relationships			
Constructive communications			
Raising awareness of alternative thinking strategies			

Positivity in the future

When the media and many soap operas focus on the negative, and headlines routinely announce the worst of human behaviour, there is a risk that people will begin to believe that this is the norm. They perceive 'human nature' as greedy, selfish, aggressive and doom-laden. This can lead to suspicion of others, expectation that we will be treated badly, and a temptation to get in first. This is a recipe for misery and mayhem, and we can already see elements of this on social media, if not in public and political arenas.

But reality paints a different picture. Cruelty and callousness are not the most common ways of being, because when it comes to psychological stability, let alone survival, we need each other. There are plenty of examples – and evidence – that many individuals are kind, considerate, honourable, generous, empathic and grateful for the good things – especially for the healthy, supportive relationships that are at the heart of wellbeing.

We might be forgiven for thinking that altruism and other positive social values are going out of fashion, but they are as relevant to wellbeing as they have ever been. Perhaps for our children to thrive and experience a hopeful future, these values need to be brought out into the light and become more central in education. Positivity in all its diverse manifestations needs to colour our conversations, be threaded through our actions, and celebrated in as many spheres as possible, especially in every classroom, every day.

References, further reading and resources

Burson, S.R. & Castelli, D.M. (2022). How Elementary In-School Play Opportunities Relate to Academic Achievement and Social-Emotional Well-Being: Systematic Review. *Journal of School Health*, 92(10), 945–958.

Dweck, C.S. (2017). *Mindset - Updated Edition: Changing The Way You think To Fulfil Your Potential*. Random House.

Fredrickson, B.L. (2013). Positive emotions broaden and build. In E. Ashby Plant & P.G. Devine (Eds.), *Advances on Experimental Social Psychology*, 47, 1–53. Academic Press.

Fredrickson, B.L. (2001). The role of positive emotions in positive psychology. The broaden-and-build theory of positive emotions. *American Psychologist*, 56(3), 218–226.

Gray, P. (2011). The decline of play and the rise of psychopathology in children and adolescents. *American Journal of Play*, 3(4), 443–463.

Grenville-Cleave, B. & Boniwell, I. (2012). Surviving or thriving? Do teachers have lower perceived control and well-being than other professions? *Management in Education*, 26(1), 3–5.

Hoyle, T. (2021). *101 Playground Games – A collection of Active and Engaging Games for Children* 2nd Edition. Routledge.

Montessori, M. (1988). *The Montessori Method, Rev'd Ed*. Knopf Doubleday.

New South Wales Commission for Children and Young People. (2002–9). *Ask the Children*. Although the Commission and its website no longer exist, the National Library of Australia archived copies of the relevant pages in 2010, which can be accessed here: https://webarchive.nla.gov.au/tep/116783

O'Brien, M. & Blue, L. (2018). Towards a positive pedagogy: designing pedagogical practices that facilitate Positivity within the classroom. *Educational Action Research*, 26(3), 365–384.

Petersen, C., Maier, S.F. & Seligman, M.E.P. (1995). *Learned Helplessness: A Theory for the Age of Personal Control*. Oxford University Press

Petersen, C. & Seligman, M.E.P. (2004). *Character Strengths and Virtues: A Handbook of Classification*. OUP.

Roffey, S. (2011). *Changing Behaviour in Schools: Promoting Positive Relationships and Wellbeing*. Sage.

Seligman, M.E.P. (2006). *Learned Optimism: How to Change Your Mind and Your Life*. Vintage Books.

Tidmund, L. (2021). Building Positive emotions and Playfulness. In M.L. Kern & M.L. Weymeher (Eds.), *The Palgrave Handbook of Positive Education*.

Other sources and further reading

Gill, T.R. (2007). *No Fear - Growing Up in a Risk Averse Society.* This is now out of print, but a full copy can be downloaded at: https://timrgill.files.wordpress.com/2010/10/no-fear-19-12-07.pdf

Gottman, J., Schwartz Gottman, J., & DeClaire, J. (2006). *10 Lessons to Transform Your Marriage.* Crown Publishers.

Hascher, T. & Waber, J. (2021). Teacher well-being: A systematic review of the research literature from the year 2000–2019. *Educational Research Review, 34*(2021), Article 100411.

Hattie, J. (2008). *Visible Learning: A Synthesis of Over 800 Meta-analyses Relating to Achievement.* Routledge.

Hattie, J. (2023). *Visible Learning: The Sequel. A Synthesis of Over 2,100 Meta-analyses Relating to Achievement.* Routledge.

Howells, K. (2012). *Gratitude in Education: A Radical View.* Sense Publishers.

McCallum, F. (2021). Teacher and Staff Wellbeing: Understanding the Experiences of School Staff. In M.L. Kern & M.L. Wehmeyer, *The Palgrave Handbook of Positive Education* (open access).

McGuinness, C., Sproule, L., Bojke, C., Trew, K., & Walsh, G. (2014). Impact of a play-based curriculum in the first two years of primary school: literacy and numeracy outcomes over seven years. *British Educational Research Journal, 40*(5), 772–795.

MacLure, M., Jones, L., Holmes, R. & MacRae, C. (2012). Becoming a problem: behaviour and reputation in the early years classroom. *British Educational Research Journal, 38*(3), 447–471.

Martineau, W. & Bakopoulou, I. (2023). What children need to flourish: insights from a qualitative study of children's mental health and wellbeing in the pandemic. *Education 3–13,* 29 April 2023.

Quinlan, D., Vella-Brodrick, D.A. Gray, A. & Swain, N. (2019) Teachers matter: Student outcomes following a strengths intervention are mediated by teacher strengths spotting. *Journal of Happiness Studies, 20,* 2507–2523.

Roffey, S. & Hromek, R. (2009). Games as a pedagogy to promote social and emotional learning: 'It's fun and we learn things'. *Simulation and Gaming, 40*(5), 626–644.

Roffey, S. (Ed) (2012a). *Positive Relationships: Evidence-based practice across the world.* Springer.

Roffey, S. (2012b). Pupil wellbeing: Teacher wellbeing: Two sides of the same coin? *Educational and Child Psychology, 29*(4), 817.

Roffey, S. (2017). Ordinary magic' needs ordinary magicians: The power and practice of positive relationships for building youth resilience and wellbeing. *Kognition und Paedagogik Social Resiliens, 103,* 38–57. Available in English at https://www.growinggreatschoolsworldwide.com/publications/articles/

Singh, N. & Duraiappah, A.K. (2021). *Building Kinder Brains.* UNESCO MGIEP.

Resources

Healthy Child Development: Centre for the Developing Child https://www.developingchild.harvard.edu/

Relationships: https://www.childline.org.uk/info-advice/friends-relationships-sex/friends/top-tips-making-friends/

BucketFillingActivities:https://www.proudtobeprimary.com/bucket-filler-activities-for-the-classroom/ This site includes books, videos and activities.

Emotions: Sesame Street Belly Breathe https://www.youtube.com/watch?v=_mZbzDOpylA

Play

Centre for the Developing Child – booklets on play activities for children at different ages: https://www.developingchild.harvard.edu/resources/brainbuildingthroughplay/

The importance of play – a video from the British Psychological Society: https://www.youtube.com/watch?v=d9wjcE7elwg

Making playtime an important part of the school day: https://www.outdoorclassroomday.org.uk/wp-content/uploads/sites/2/2016/06/ECD-Making-Playtime-a-Key-Part-of-the-School-Day.pdf
https://www.theresehoyle.com/free-playground-games/

Positive Thinking

Blog in *Education Week*: Carol Dweck revisits the growth mindset: https://www.edweek.org/leadership/opinion-carol-dweck-revisits-the-growth-mindset/2015/09
The Wellbeing Stories put different types of thinking into characters – e.g. the If-Only Elf and the Beautiful Blessings. There are six illustrated stories with a teacher toolkit and a family toolkit for each. The teacher toolkit has activities to do in class and the family toolkit says more about the issues – such as transition to high school, loss and living in two families. See https://www.wellbeing stories.com, where you can download a free introduction.

4 Inclusion

Everyone welcome, everyone matters,
everyone participates

What do we mean by Inclusion?

Inclusion is a universal human right. It is seeing each individual as worthy of both respect and participation. It is not simply tolerating difference but accepting and celebrating each person's unique place in the world and also valuing our shared humanity – that we have more in common than divides us. It does not discriminate against anyone on account of their gender, race, sexuality, disability, religion, socio-economic status, ethnicity, idiosyncrasy or anything else. It challenges the definition of what is 'normal' and embraces the diversity that enriches us all. This chapter does not specify how to include different groups but details the principle of Inclusion and associated practices that apply to everyone, everywhere.

Although the continuums of inclusion/exclusion, school connectedness/rejection and belonging/alienation are discrete constructs, they are interdependent. For the purposes of this chapter, the first applies to actions taken at a school level; the second is what happens for individuals in a specific context; the last is a feeling that can powerfully affect a student's perception of themselves and their attitudes to school, teachers and learning.

Inclusive policies and practices are not just focused on those at risk of discrimination but the way all stakeholders in a school think about and treat each other. This is why you will find empathy in this chapter rather than in the one on positivity. Inclusion as a principle in positive education impacts on everyone, both in the learning environment and the future we are creating.

Belonging

We are hard-wired to connect with others. Babies do not smile at 6 weeks by accident; it enhances their chances of survival by positively engaging with – and rewarding – those who are caring for them. We all need to feel we belong somewhere. It is critical to our psychological and emotional wellbeing and is now known as one of the main factors for resilience and positive adaptation to adversity.

Most people feel they belong within their family – and in my experience, even children who have been badly treated by their parents will still fiercely defend them. Other places people might have a sense of belonging are in a school, sports club, faith group, friendship group, local gang, youth club, political party, neighbourhood, city or nation. There are also communities of shared interests and professions, some of which are online. Belonging is along a continuum – you are closer to some people than others, and it depends on context – what is happening at the time and how engaged you are with others. Cheering your team along with others on a Saturday afternoon can make you feel part of something highly significant!

There are, however, two aspects to belonging, and the difference is important.

DOI: 10.4324/9781003428237-5

Exclusive belonging

Exclusive belonging is where you are attached to a closed group. Being inside such a group can be protective and make you feel your presence matters, so it can be positive for mental health, at least on the surface. It can provide reciprocal support and a sense of solidarity. But closed groups may be dominated by powerful individuals who establish and monitor the criteria for belonging. If you follow their rules, all may be well, but deviation can place you outside – either temporarily or for good.

Exclusive groups often maintain a sense of superiority over those who are outsiders and in some cases treat them as unworthy – even subhuman. Putnam (2000) refers to exclusive groups as demonstrating 'bonding' social capital bound by the sociological equivalent of super-glue. Tight-knit, inflexible and maybe self-congratulatory, they can position other people outside the group as objects, having little concern or compassion for anyone not part of their community, an attitude he calls an 'I-it' orientation. This is most evident in strict religions or nationalistic governments. It was the basis of apartheid and the Holocaust and is evident wherever politicians and/or the military stir up emotions against one group of people, facilitating cruelty and even genocide. You also find this exclusivity in online networks that reinforce each other's views, however damaging and erroneous these may be. People sometimes refer to these individuals as being in a 'bubble' where a certain sense of reality is shared, strengthened and resists challenge, maybe demonising those who try. We need to teach children to be critical thinkers so that they are aware of how false information is spread, and they can choose to make decisions about their lives based on the evidence of what is real. Awareness of emotional manipulation and contagion may also help prevent exploitation and perhaps succumbing to peer pressure.

Leaving an exclusive group, especially if your identity is tied up with its norms and values, is a risk to stability, sense of self and support. It is only when something happens that deeply confronts a person's sense of who they are that they might consider this. Some individuals leave their families or exclusive communities to escape the restrictions imposed on them, perhaps over sexuality, authoritarian traditions or a conflict of values, but unless they are welcomed and accepted by others, they may experience overwhelming loneliness and a challenge to their mental health and wellbeing.

Inclusive belonging

Inclusive belonging, on the other hand, is open to all. It values diversity and welcomes everyone. People do not quickly jump to judgment about individuals based on stereotypes and prejudice but instead show interest and seek understanding for an 'I-you' orientation where shared humanity is at the forefront of decisions. Putnam refers to this as 'bridging' social capital, the sociological equivalent of WD-40 – the lubricating substance used on metal machine parts to keep them moving and not getting stuck. An inclusive approach oils the wheels of relationships between groups, such as home and school. Inclusive belonging fosters healthy relationships and high social capital, making collaboration towards agreed goals more likely.

Some may see this as idealistic, but there is now a wealth of research (e.g. Philpot et al., 2020; Vlerick, 2021) that indicates that altruism and kindness towards others are part of the human condition and often enhance happiness and wellbeing (Post, 2005). Empathy is reliably aroused in humans in response to misfortune in others but mediated by how we think about others and the situation they are in. We may not see much empathy in people with power at the macro-level of an ecological framework, but there are always those who will stand up for others and intervene to protect them when and where they can.

Inclusion can, however, be challenging, as it asks for privileged individuals and groups to relinquish some of what they have in order for distribution of resources to be fairer. This is likely be resisted until people realise that in the end everyone benefits. We never know when we might need Inclusion to apply to us or the people we love.

Mattering

Isaac Prilleltensky has written extensively on 'mattering' (2020, 2021). He defines this as feeling valued but also being of value – making a recognised contribution. It is a feeling that you count, can make a difference, are trusted to do so and that authentic opportunities are available. This is highly relatable across geographic and cultural boundaries.

Feeling valued begins in infancy with healthy attachment to primary carers. It then broadens out to a sense of belonging to a wider group – family, then community.

> *Dignity is the backbone of mattering ... it is the quality of being worthy, honoured and esteemed. ... It is the feeling of being recognised, acknowledged, included and respected for who we are or what we know ... making us feel human.*
>
> (Prilleltensky, 2021 p 32)

However, being valued is not enough to fully matter. To add value, we need to contribute. Adding value to enhance our lives personally can include learning, finding and following a passion or purpose, working towards a goal, or developing confidence in new competencies. Adding value to our communities can include emotional, physical, psychological or practical support. It can be positive communication with others, helping, sharing, listening, being part of a team project, having a role in sporting or social events or volunteering. In schools all children need opportunities to add value – this is aligned with the principle of Agency.

Belonging to school

What does it mean to belong to your school? In 1993, Goodenow and Grady defined this as *"the extent to which students feel personally accepted, respected, included, and supported by others in the school social environment"*. It is also now acknowledged that school belonging is also aligned with purpose and progress in learning. Unless students can appreciate the relevance to their own lives of what is on the curriculum and perceive themselves as making progress, school as a hub of knowledge and understanding has little meaning for them.

The Wingspread Declaration on School Connections (2004) identified four factors that influence school connectedness. These are: adult support; belonging to positive peer groups; commitment to education; and the quality of the school environment. Relationships are central. Students are more likely to feel they belong to school when they believe that the adults there are interested in them as people, care about their learning and help them aim high. Teachers who try to make learning contextually relevant are also promoting a sense of belonging. Pupils disengage when learning is neither meaningful nor challenging, so it is unsurprising that researchers (Stevens et al., 2007) found that the more teachers encouraged ideas, supported goal-setting and mastery, asked pupils to explain their work, and promoted learning over performance, the more students felt they belonged to their school.

Students also need to have friends they can rely on and feel safe. Children who are bullied by others because they are positioned as 'different' not only have a miserable time in school, but the impact of this behaviour can have long-lasting consequences for their mental health and wellbeing. All pupils need opportunities to discuss together and reflect on how they treat each other. This is one reason why social and emotional learning needs to be at the core of education. There is more on addressing bullying in the chapter on Safety.

Why does Inclusion matter?

Congruence with the United Nations Convention on the Rights of the Child

Article 2: Non-discrimination: The Convention applies to every child without discrimination, whatever their ethnicity, sex, religion, language, abilities or any other status, whatever they think or say, whatever their family background.

A sense of belonging to school is considered fundamental to students' healthy development. It has multiple benefits, including academic motivation and engagement, prosocial behaviour, reduced anxiety, stronger mental health and resilience, positive links with families and community and constructive peer relationships – reducing the incidence of bullying behaviours. Inclusive belonging in school also has implications for society beyond the immediate learning environment, potentially addressing racism, homophobia, misogyny and discrimination against minorities. Importantly, when children and young people feel alienated from school they will look for a sense of belonging elsewhere, and are therefore potentially unsafe and vulnerable to exploitation.

School attendance and life trajectories

There is growing concern about increases in exclusions, alienation, and a sense of 'not belonging' in school, and the impact of this on young people's well-being and life chances. In the UK, research indicates that 1 in 4 pupils do not feel they belong in school, and this number increases with those from more disadvantaged communities, black pupils and those identified as having special educational needs. Four times as many black children are excluded in the UK as others, and a similar picture is evident with Aboriginal students – especially boys – in Australia. This is mirrored in statistics about later incarceration, with 25 times more indigenous youth than non-indigenous youth finding themselves in prison. Excluding students from school may give short term relief to teachers, but it has considerable implications for the life trajectory of those who miss out.

The impact of the Covid-19 pandemic on school attendance has been widely reported. There are estimates that the number of children in the UK who are more out of school than in has increased by 108%, with one in five children regularly absent. Those most at risk are children whose families are struggling with debt or homelessness, those with health issues or are carers for family members and those with additional needs. High levels of anxiety also contribute, as well as practices such as informally 'off-rolling' students who present with difficulties and/or lower a school's academic results. Although chronic absenteeism is more a feature of secondary than primary school, it remains a concern that younger children are missing out, so much so that nine special hubs have been set up in the UK to support 600 primary schools.

The concern is not just about children missing education but also their invisibility and whether anyone is monitoring their safety. We hear grim stories about some children 'falling through the net' and experiencing abuse and exploitation.

Forcing children to go to school or punishing their parents for non-compliance, however, undermines the strong, supportive relationships that foster belonging and motivate children to want to be there.

In *Square Pegs* (Morgan & Costello, 2023) we read about many children and young people who are simply unable to go to school. They don't fit in. This has been traditionally considered a problem within the child – something is wrong with them. Alternatively, they are labelled as being non-compliant and potentially delinquent 'truants'. The push/pull analysis, once a popular conceptual framework for non-attendance is now seen as limited. The pull factors are things going on at home or in the community perceived as more important than school such as bereavement, family violence or mental health concerns. The push factors are what is happening at school that makes pupils not want to be there, such as bullying or constant pressure to perform. Environmental and social issues have had less attention but are also powerful. This includes poverty, transport, political policies, school priorities and access to support, especially for children with special educational needs and disabilities. Schools that are inflexible with a 'one-size-fits-all' approach are unable to cater for these pupils. When square pegs do not fit in round holes, we need to make square holes.

The organisation 'Not Fine in School' was set up to provide a resource and support to families where pupils experience attendance problems and barriers. At the time of writing the Facebook group has nearly 43,000 followers. Dr Beth Bodycote interviewed members of this organisation on the problems and barriers to school attendance they had encountered and what helped. This is a brief summary of what helps:

- A resolution is more likely to be achieved when a pupil has early access to help.
- Parental concerns are too often dismissed and need to be taken seriously.
- It is valuable to work towards a shared understanding of the child's difficulties.
- Authorising absence for both physical or mental health issues, and giving support where possible, relieves the fear of blame and possible legal action.
- Teachers who respect parental knowledge of their child, acknowledge their own limitations, show empathy, and have a focus on the child's wellbeing, contribute to a positive working relationship with families.
- Parents are often in genuine need of advice and systemic support, not dismissal, judgment or condemnation.
- Children are empowered by having some control of the situation, so they have the flexibility to make small steps of progress with minimal pressure
- Helping children stay in touch with others may support a successful return.
- Measures need to be put in place to effectively address bullying.
- Providing schoolwork to do at home relieves the pressure of 'catching up'
- Regular, reliable and positive communication between home and school helps maintain positive relationships.
- Making prompt referrals to services and for assessment.
- Local authorities need to be consistent in complying with legislation for 'education other than at school' and special needs and disability (SEND)
- Patience – these issues are complex and resolution takes time – and sometimes experimentation.

The pressures on children and families often become untenable with escalating levels of stress. This negatively affects relationships, mental health, family functioning and even finances, as someone has to be at home with the child. Things only improve when parents accept the situation and begin to prioritise their child's wellbeing above compliance with authorities and cultural expectations. Mainstream school is not for everyone, and academic success is not the only way to a life well lived.

Case-study: Josh

Josh was a 6-year-old who had come down to London from the north of England with his mother, the parents having split up. His older sister in junior school was doing well, but Josh was of great concern. His teacher said that he did not settle well to learning and was often not compliant with instruction. She said he disturbed other children and was generally quite 'naughty'. Josh had stopped wanting to go to school and did everything he possibly could to stay away, feigning illness, locking himself in the bathroom and refusing to get dressed. His mother was at her wit's end, but the teacher made it quite clear that it was the parent's fault he wasn't attending and that it was her responsibility to get him to school, even if she had to force him physically. The whole family were in a state of great distress, and Josh's mum was reluctant to go anywhere near the school herself. But then a new term began with a different teacher. She made a point of finding out about Josh, what he liked, what interested him and asked him what she could do to help him feel better about coming to school. When Josh's mum was asked to come to school to see the new teacher, she was initially fearful of what would be said but came away feeling respected and hopeful. Within a few weeks, Josh had settled and was beginning to make progress, bringing home little certificates which told his mother what he had achieved that day – not just in maths and reading but including such things as playing with a new friend.

It is likely that Josh had been affected more than anyone realised by his parents' separation. Unless this is mediated for children under the age of 7, they often think it is somehow their fault – and are anxious that they might lose the other parent as well. They are often confused, fearful and sometimes angry. They need a great deal of reassurance. But the strongest factor in resolving this situation was a teacher who focused on what would help, asked good questions and made Josh (and his mum) feel OK about coming to school.

Feelings of rejection

In the Positivity chapter we talk about the importance of positive feelings in the classroom and how these promote cognitive skills and prosocial behaviours. This is even more important when we consider the implications of negative feelings.

Exclusion and rejection are powerful instigators of emotions that can have far-reaching consequences. Social rejection activates many of the same brain regions involved in physical pain, and it is now acknowledged that the pain of being excluded is on a par with that of physical hurt. Social rejection can influence not only mental health but also cognition and even physical health. It may also have wider and more dangerous implications, leading to aggression and even violence. In 2003, Leary and colleagues analysed 15 cases of school shooters and found all but two suffered from social rejection.

When someone is included by a group and feels they belong there they are more likely to see this community as important to them, cooperate with others and abide by behaviours expected to stay connected.

Resilience and mental health

Resilience is the ability to cope with and thrive in the face of one or more negative life events, whereas positive adaptation refers to how someone might respond to chronic adverse experiences in ways that enhance a positive sense of self and healthy relationships. The latter is, of course, much harder to achieve. Research has shown that there are both personal and environmental factors that increase the chances of doing well despite severe challenges and that one of these is feeling you belong. The others are having someone who believes in the best of you and has high expectations of what you might do and who you might become. All these are encapsulated in high-quality teacher-student relationships. Teachers can make more difference than they realise, and it would be valuable if policymakers acknowledged how much this matters to both wellbeing and learning.

Behaviour

When children feel respected as part of the school community, they are much more likely to want to stay connected – and their behaviour will often reflect this. They may still have triggering moments when they are out of control but will be more remorseful afterwards and willing, if not eager, to 'restore' their connection. See *restorative approaches* in this chapter.

Inclusion in practice in the early years

The books that are presented to young children and how adults talk about the stories will make a difference to how others are perceived. There are now many excellent books, some of which are listed in the resources, that provide a stimulus for conversations about kindness, fairness and Inclusion in the early years setting. A notable one, now made into an animated film and also a stage play, is *The Smeds and the Smoos*, cartoon characters who look different and have ways of being that the other group denigrates. This is from the film promotion:

> *Bill and Janet fall in love while their families are at war. Faced with disapproval, they flee to a distant planet and Grandma Smoo and Grandpa Smed must put aside their differences and work together to bring them back home.*

Children who see and hear about different ethnicities, various disabilities and diverse families in stories will not only feel represented themselves but also be less likely to develop prejudice against others. Although most young children readily accept difference, countering the seeds of discrimination at an early age may help to maintain values of Inclusion as children grow and may be influenced by other, more negative conversations.

Expectations about interactions also establish understanding about how to be with others. Children need to learn basic social skills of sharing and taking turns, but here is another tool in the promotion of positive relationships and Inclusion.

You Can't Say You Can't Play

In the early years, fostering inclusion and belonging is crucial to creating a nurturing learning environment. Vivian Paley offers a practical example of how educators can promote these values in practice. In her seminal book (1993), Paley introduces a simple but powerful instruction: "*You Can't Say You Can't Play.*" By implementing this in the early years, Paley observed a shift in the children's interactions and their sense of inclusion. The clearly stated expectation encourages young children to be more inclusive, as they learn to navigate their social world. By preventing exclusion, children are more likely to form connections with peers and develop empathy for those who they might not usually play with. This may foster a sense of belonging within the classroom, as every child feels valued and welcome in all play activities.

A second strategy to foster belonging is allowing transitional toys or objects from home, which can provide comfort and a sense of familiarity to children as they adjust to their new surroundings. Inclusion is deeply contextual, and practitioners must find what works best for them. Balancing the needs of children with the demands of the educational environment can be challenging, but it is crucial to prioritise strategies that genuinely support a sense of belonging for every child from their earliest years in school.

Associate Professor Kelly-Ann Allen, belonging researcher at Monash University, Australia.

Welcoming families

The nuclear family of a married mum and dad and two or three children living in the same household is no longer the norm – and for many cultures it has never been so. Families have a wide range of structures, and most early years professionals acknowledge and take account of this. But the images presented to children in books, stories, cards, celebrations and media also need to represent this diversity. When families first register their child, it helps to ask routine questions that enable staff to have contextual understanding of who is in a child's life at home to ensure everyone feels welcome and accepted.

Inclusion in practice in the primary classroom

It is the relationships that pupils have with teachers and peers that most strongly mediate feelings of belonging. It is not just sharing the same space that matters but whether or not these relationships are warm, accepting, supportive and fair. Micro-moments matter. The words that are said, as well as simple actions, can be momentary, but when they happen on a regular basis, they provide the foundation for pupils to feel their presence is welcomed and valued. The way teachers interact with students – and also with each other – provides a model for how students should be with each other.

Teacher-student relationships

Simply greeting students by name in the morning and smiling, looking pleased to see them, can significantly increase a sense of belonging. Not bearing grudges and seeing every day as a new day also helps.

A simple intervention that involved teachers and students finding out five commonalities they shared reduced the achievement gap in one school by an astonishing 60% (Gehlbach et al., 2016). This is easily replicable in schools and clearly worth doing.

Teaching and learning

Supportive teachers consider different learning levels and keep students' views in mind when conducting and scaffolding activities in the classroom. This enables pupils to engage more fully with learning and perceive themselves as making progress. Positive psychologist Mihalyi Csikszentmihalyi (2002) writes about the concept of 'flow' as the moment in which individuals are at their happiest and most engaged. In schools this would equate to where a pupil has enough prior learning to tune into the subject, so they see any challenge presented as building on their knowledge base and therefore achievable. This aligns with intrinsic motivation. Where something is entirely outside a pupil's frame of reference they may be confused, anxious and possibly switched off. If the material presented is too easy or overly repetitive, then there is a risk of boredom. Another educational pioneer, Vygotsky (1978), talked about learning happening in 'the zone of proximal development', which is a similar conceptual framework to 'flow'.

Meeting the needs of diverse learners in a class is clearly a highly demanding task for teachers when they are expected to deliver the same curriculum content regardless. There here are, however, recommendations on ways to maximise engagement with learning: Most educators will already be familiar with these.

1 Reducing distractions from the learning experience itself, such as tests and rules
2 Identifying, acknowledging and fostering pupil interests and strengths
3 Clarifying the goals of the task so pupils know what they are aiming for. For some pupils this means breaking down a task into smaller steps so that they are not overwhelmed and see the task as achievable
4 Providing specific feedback on what has been achieved and the next step
5 Encouraging self-evaluation. *"What was good about that piece of work?"* *"What could you do better?"* *"What help do you need?"*
6 Asking pupils to give feedback to teachers on what sense they have made of the task.

'Personal bests' is a concept well known in the sporting world and has potential in the classroom, as pupils competing against themselves cannot be losers! It reduces competition with others and enables pupils to take pride in their own achievements.

Co-operative and project-based learning enables pupils to learn from each other and be stimulated by new ideas. Vygotsky emphasised the value of social interactions in learning and the potential of peer support.

Peer relationships

When children are getting ready to go to school, the chances are that they are not so much looking forward to a specific lesson but to spending time with their friends. Some children, however, may wonder whether they will have people to play with. The social dynamics of a class may need active intervention to ensure everyone is included.

Children in primary school can be cruel to those they perceive as different, especially if they have not had educational input that values diversity. This may be instigated by a child who needs to feel important and in control. As there is often a gender divide in the primary classroom, with girls more likely to be engaged in small communicative groups and boys in larger, activity-based groups, exclusion can be the way a 'queen bee' maintains power. This needs addressing at a whole-class level before such bullying behaviour destroys someone's self-esteem.

Regularly mixing pupils up so that they work with everyone else in the class and get to know them can help develop knowledge and understanding of individuals and reduce stereotyping. It can be humiliating for children when they are not picked as a partner or team member – especially if this happens regularly – so finding other ways of doing this, either randomly or teacher-led, can ensure no child feels marginalised.

Empathy

Including others requires empathy – being able to tune into others and their needs. Some children in warm, supportive families learn to do this from an early age, but that is not the case for every pupil. Some need to discover what empathy means, both by experiencing it and having opportunities to learn and develop it. One innovative way of doing this, Roots of Empathy, originated in Canada but has been successful all over the world (Schonert-Reichl et al., 2012).

Roots of Empathy is solidly based on scientific knowledge of the human condition ... it takes us into the pedagogy of how one can develop and foster attachment, emotional literacy, authentic communication and social inclusion.

(Emeritus Professor Education Michael Fullan)

Roots of Empathy

This classroom-based program is for children aged 5–13.

A baby visits a classroom throughout the school year with their parent(s), along with a trained Roots of Empathy Instructor. The children are coached to recognize and connect with the vulnerability and humanity of the baby. Through guided observation, they label the baby's feelings and intentions, learning the affective aspect of empathy (emotion) and the cognitive aspect of empathy (perspective-taking).

Emotional literacy develops as children begin to identify and label the baby's feelings, reflect on and understand their own feelings, then link this to understand the feelings of others. The Instructor also visits the classroom the week before and the week after the family visit to prepare for and then reflect on the activities of the family visit. These pre and post visits deepen the development of emotional literacy, helping children to understand how their behaviour or words can hurt others. This enables pupils to build connections and healthy relationships which lead to Inclusion and integration.

Inclusion in practice across the primary school

Although individual teachers can do a lot to support a sense of belonging with the young people they interact with on a regular basis, this will not be sustainable across years unless Inclusion is prioritised across the whole school. There is no blueprint, as each school is operating within a different context and senior leadership teams will need to liaise with stakeholders to establish the most effective ways of doing this.

A meta-analysis of 51 studies (Allen et al., 2018) identified many individual and social level factors that influence school belonging. These core themes include academic factors, personal characteristics, social relationships, demographic characteristics, school climate and extracurricular activities. For many of the determinants of school belonging, University College, the Institute of Education and the National Teachers Union (Riley, Coates & Allen, 2020) researched place and belonging in school and identified three interconnected themes that underpinned intentional positive school practice:

- Leadership creates culture.
- Culture shapes learning and behaviour.
- Together, these shape agency and belonging.

Case-study

In Flakesfleet Primary School, one in three children is living in poverty, leading to loss of identity, low expectations and poor self-belief. The school focused on changing learning and teaching, shaping expectations and the culture of the school. The emphasis was on what children could do, not on what they were not allowed to do. Staff set out to model desired behaviours and attitudes, such as working together and respecting each other. The other key piece of the jigsaw was 'Dare to Dream': about envisioning the 'impossible' and making it happen – skydiving, achieving a Christmas number one song, winning 'Britain's Got Talent'. The headteacher thought it vital to change the children's beliefs about what is possible and showcase the results. The staff feel that they belong in the school and are valued: 'part of the place'. They are committed to translating pupils' dreams into realities. In the research interviews, children found it hard to recall any place or incident within the school where they felt they did not belong. The school is a joyous place to be. The children are engaged, results are rising and numbers are growing. And although they didn't win Britain's Got Talent, they did get to the final!

Community and home relationships

Notices, directions and labels across a school need to be the languages of those communities that the school serves. Posters on the walls that reflect achievements of people that look like the pupils in the school are more likely to motivate them. This includes female scientists, engineers and bus drivers and male nurses and carers, as well as a diverse range of ethnicities, especially those the school serves.

The relationship between school and home is a two-way street, but the initiative to promote Inclusion begins with the school. Asking for involvement in an open and general way is less likely to help families feel connected than if schools request specific support that values their culture. This could include:

- Asking parents about games they played as children that could be taught to pupils
- Seeing if families would come and make traditional food with groups of children, with support from a teaching assistant
- Asking for advice about cultural celebrations and involving community groups in leading school activities
- Inviting families to share stories with children in class
- Putting out requests for practical help when appropriate, such as teams to develop a school garden
- Ensuring communities are represented on governing bodies and parent groups.

The school being visible in the community also helps, such as being present at local festivities. Continually reviewing community relations is vital as groups move on to be replaced by different individuals.

World Café

World Café is a way of sharing knowledge, generating ideas and constructing dialogues with groups. Although more commonly used with students, this is a way of involving parents and community in the life of the school and getting their views on specific issues. It provides an opportunity to matter by contributing to discussion and being of value.

Participants are sent an invitation which gives options for days and times. Several World Cafés may be offered, to include as many families and communities as possible. It may be necessary to translate invitations and engage translators.

Families are welcomed by the facilitator, who explains the process and encourages the discussion to be positive, solution-focused and respectful to all – even when disagreeing.

Parents sit four or five to a table and discuss the question(s) they have been given. Examples might be:

• What helps children feel they belong to school?
• What helps families feel connected to this school?
• What else would help?

   One person on the table keeps a note of what is said. You can choose to have a different question on each table. After 20 minutes, everyone except the scribe gets up and changes tables. The idea is to mix everyone up to talk with new people. The scribe quickly summarises what was said by the first group, and then the second discussion begins.

   After another 20 minutes, there is another change, with the scribe taking the same role.

   At the end of the hour, the facilitator summarizes the discussion and thanks the families for their participation. Decisions taken by the school on the basis of these discussions are communicated to parents/communities.

Behaviour and restorative practice

Zero-tolerance behaviour policies do not work over the longer term. The American Psychological Association published the research from their Zero-Tolerance Task Force (2008) and found that not only did behaviour not improve across the school, but it worsened outcomes in learning, as there were always others to replace the students excluded. Relationships became authoritarian rather than supportive. Their recommendations include a whole of community approach and restorative practices.

Restorative practice emphasises communication, empathy, and accountability. Rather than a focus on sanctions that often exclude a student from their peers, it emphasises reconciliation and reintegration. It positions unacceptable behaviour as harm to the community and looks to resolve conflict and repair this harm. As practitioner Bill Hansberry says:

> *As communities become increasingly disconnected and fearful of one another, responses to conflict, harm and wrongdoing that bring people and their difficult emotions face to face can seem too risky, yet schools who have bravely embraced restorative practices have found that this is a risk well worth taking.*

It takes training and time to establish restorative practice, as it requires everyone in the school to understand what it entails, be supportive of the approach, and ensure that other policies and practices are compatible. It does not simply consist of a set of statements and questions. It begins with creating community, but once established is far more effective over the longer term, as it changes not just behaviour but relationships and responsibility. The aim is to maintain a sense of community by:

• Providing pathways to repair the harm done
• Bringing together everyone who has been affected in a dialogue that works towards achieving a common understanding
• Coming to an agreement about resolving the conflict and moving forward.

Restorative approaches can be seen as part of a broader ethos or culture that identifies strong, mutually respectful relationships and a cohesive community as the foundations on which good teaching and learning can flourish.

School uniform

The issue of uniform in school is controversial, and advocates for either having or not having one are often strongly committed to their position. Like many things, it is not just what pupils wear that matters but what it represents and how uniform policy is implemented. Wearing the same outfit as others might indicate the school a pupil attends but does not promote a sense of belonging unless that individual is already proud and pleased to be associated with the school. For those who feel alienated, it can be something to either tolerate or resist. A major problem is a focus on uniform infringements. When pupils are singled out or given sanctions for not having the right length socks (this really happened to a 5-year-old!), a poorly knotted tie or 'inappropriate shoes', this can undermine positive relationships and a sense of belonging. The more specific and detailed the uniform requirements are, the more expensive for parents and the more opportunities for critical conversations. Alternatives to that could include students wearing jeans of their choice and a T-shirt with the school's name or a recommendation for a simple colour code – such as everyone wearing red and grey. Trousers for all reduces the safety concerns posed by skirt length.

Inclusion in social and emotional learning (SEL)

The Inclusion principle in Circle Solutions is activated by regularly mixing students up so that they talk with those outside their usual social circle. Doing this in a variety of games makes it harder for pupils to try and stay close to friends. As Circles continue over time, however, getting to know others they wouldn't normally talk to becomes something students look forward to and enjoy. This in itself promotes connection and inhibits prejudice and stereotyping. As teachers are full participants in Circle Solutions they also find out more about their pupils in these activities, fostering positive relationships and understanding.

Activities in SEL

These not only explore how we think about others but also aim to promote interest and understanding of the values of good relationships. It is important that the teacher is aware of the context of their class so that they do not inadvertently raise issues that are especially difficult for some.

Pair shares:

Finding what partners have in common – everyone having the same conversation. This can include facts about their lives, what they like or don't like and what they think about an issue; for example:

– What they both like/hate to eat
– Sports they both enjoy – either playing or watching
– A funny cartoon/film/program they have both seen
– What cheers them both up when they are feeling upset
– Someone they both admire and look up to and why.

The teacher can then go round the Circle – perhaps using a talking stick to indicate whose turn it is – with the pairs beginning a sentence "We both …"
    It is fine for pairs to repeat what others have said – this again shows commonalities.

Paired interviews:

This is each partner finding out about the other. It is the basis of good conversations – showing interest, asking good questions, listening to the answers and taking it in turns to speak. Topics given by the teacher can be expanded but might include:

- Family celebrations
- Random act of kindness
- Favourite book
- A long journey
- My earliest memory

There are hundreds of topics to choose from but also many useful resources to help busy teachers.

Small group/whole-class activities

Strengths in Circles Cards

There are seven statements for each of the six ASPIRE principles.
  These are four of those for Inclusion

* We accept each other.
* We work with everyone.
* We welcome everyone.
* We invite contributions.

In groups of three or four students, take one statement at a time and discuss the following questions together.

- What does this mean? What would we see and hear?
- Is this what we want in our class?
- What would it make people feel about being here?
- Is it already happening – how do we know?
- What else might we do?

Each group decides on one action. They give a brief report back to the Circle, emphasising the action. What they all agree is put on display as a reminder.

Hypothetical:

A student volunteers to reads out a brief story about a fictional pupil in a particular situation. This is one about including a pupil who has cerebral palsy.

My name is Logan. I have cerebral palsy, so although I enjoy learning, my speech is not very clear, especially when I am anxious. When I walk, I am stiff and a bit wobbly. No one is unkind to me, but no one speaks to me much either. I am on my own a lot.

The pupils work in groups of three or four. They are asked these questions one at a time:

- How would you feel if you were Logan?
- What would you want to happen?
- What is one thing this group could do to help?
- Write a sentence you can say to Logan and one of the group comes and says it to the person who read the story.

The last action is important, as it puts theory into action – this is often left out so that actual practice does not change. The class now has some ideas of how to include someone who is different – ideas they have developed themselves rather than being told by the teacher.

Not jumping to judgment:

(This activity is best suited to upper primary)

Small groups of three to four pupils are given an envelope with a picture on the front of something that might belong to a child. This might be a toy, a pet, an item for sport or a hobby or something they have just found, such as a feather or a shell. The group spends a couple of minutes talking about the item and what this might tell them about the person who owns it. In the envelope are three statements that say more about the person, such as: *She is a refugee. He helps his father every Saturday at their market stall. They are the youngest of seven children and live with their grandmother. She loves music.* The group takes out one at a time and then discusses how this statement might make them see the person differently.

At the end of the activity, the groups are asked to talk about what they learnt by doing this activity and what difference it might make to how they see people in the future.

Inclusion checklist

INCLUSION	This is in place – we know it is effective because …	Working on it – our actions to date are …	Just started – our next step will be …
Welcome and support in place for new pupils			
Asking children what helps them feel they belong			
Asking children what helps them to learn			
Notices/directions in community languages			
School celebrates community festivals			
SEL activities to value diversity and promote Inclusion			
Restorative approaches to behaviour			
Time protected for teachers to get to know pupils			
Friendship/Inclusion activities that inhibit bullying behaviours			
Flexible responses for pupils who are struggling with attendance			

Inclusion in the future

If we are going to build a healthier, safer, more cohesive society, we need to ensure that children feel they belong to school and see themselves thriving there. We need to teach and model the value of diversity and our shared humanity. This includes honouring the unique value of every child, whatever their ability, background or aspiration, as well as acknowledging our commonalities.

Engaging fully with families and the community also builds the positive connections that impact on student wellbeing and learning. Community Schools make both economic and educational sense. This is not just a school run by a local authority, but where it becomes the hub of a community, open to all and providing services and support that fit each neighbourhood's needs. It is created and run by the people who live there together with school staff. Although Community Schools are not yet a feature of the UK educational landscape, they are being established elsewhere, such as in the US, where research indicates they have much to offer (Maier et al., 2017).

References, further reading and resources

Allen, K.-A., Kern, M.L., Vella-Brodrick, D.A., Hattie, J. & Waters, L. (2018). What schools need to know about fostering school belonging: A meta-Analysis. *Educational Psychology Review*, *30*(1), 1–34.

American Psychological Association Zero Tolerance Task Force. (2008). Are zero tolerance policies effective in the schools?: an evidentiary review and recommendations. *American Psychologist*, *63*(9), 852–862.

Bodycote, B. (2023). School Attendance Problems and Barriers. In F. Morgan & E. Costello (Eds.), *Square Pegs*, (35–56). Independent Thinking Press.

Csikszentmihalyi, M. (2002). *Flow: The Classic Work on How to Achieve Happiness*. Rider.

Gehlbach, H., Brinkworth, M.E., Hsu, L., King, A., McIntyre, J. & Rogers, T. (2016). Creating birds of similar feathers: Leveraging similarity to improve teacher-student relationships and academic achievement. *Journal of Educational Psychology*, *108*(3).

Goodenow, C. & Grady, K.E. (1993). The Relationship of School Belonging and Friends' Values to Academic Motivation Among Urban Adolescent Students. *The Journal of Experimental Education*, *62*(1), 60–71.

Leary, M.R., Kowalski, R.M., Smith, L. & Phillips, S. (2003). Teasing, rejection, and violence: Case studies of the school shootings. *Aggressive Behavior*, *29*(3), 202–214.

Maier, A., Daniel, J., Oakes, J. & Lam, L. (2017). *Community schools as an effective school improvement strategy: A review of the evidence*. Palo Alto, CA: Learning Policy Institute.

Morgan, F. & Costello, E. (2023). *Square Pegs: Inclusivity, compassion and fitting in. A guide for schools*. Independent Thinking Press.

Paley, V.G. (1993). *You Can't Say You Can't Play*. Harvard University Press.

Philpot, R., Liebst, L.S., Levine, M., Bernasco, W. & Lindegaard, M.R. (2020). Would I be helped? Cross-national CCTV footage shows that intervention is the norm in public conflicts. *American Psychologist*, *75*(1), 66–75.

Post, S. (2005). Altruism, Happiness, and Health: It's Good to Be Good. *International Journal of Behavioral Medicine*, *12*(2), 66–77.

Prilleltensky, I. (2020) Mattering at the intersection of psychology, philosophy and politics. *American Journal of Community Psychology*, *65*, 16–34.

Prilleltensky, I. & Prilleltensky, O. (2021). *How People Matter: Why it Affects Health, Happiness, Love, Work and Society*. Cambridge University Press.

Putnam, R.D. (2000). *Bowling alone: The Collapse and Revival of American Community*. Simon & Schuster.

Riley, K., Coates, M. & Allen, T. (2020). *Place and Belonging in School: Why it Matters Today*. Case-studies Art of Possibilities, UCL, Institute of Education, NTEU. https://www.neu.org.uk/sites/default/files/2023-04/Belongingresearchbooklet.pdf

Schonert-Reichl, K.A., Smith, V., Zaidman-Zai, A, & Hertzman, C. (2012). Promoting children's prosocial behaviors in school: Impact of the "roots of empathy" program on the social and emotional competence of school-aged children. *School Mental Health*, *4*, 1–21.

Stevens, T., Hamman, D. & Olivárez, A., Jr. (2007). Hispanic students' perception of white teachers' mastery goal orientation influences sense of school belonging. *Journal of Latinos and Education*, *6*(1), 55–70.

Vlerick, M. (2021). Explaining human altruism. *Synthese*, *199*, 2395–2413.

Vygotsky, L. S. (1978). *Mind and Society: The Development of Higher Psychological Processes*. Cambridge, MA: Harvard University Press.

Wingspread declaration on school connections. (2004). *Journal of School Health*, *74*(7), 233–234.

Other sources and further reading

Allen, K.-A., Slaten, C.D., Arslan, G., Roffey, S., Craig, H. & Vella-Brodrick, D.A. (2021). School Belonging: The Importance of Student and Teacher Relationships in M.L. Kern & M.L. Wehmeyer (Eds.), *The Palgrave Handbook of Positive Education*.

Allen, K-A. & Boyle, C. (2018). *Pathways to Belonging: Contemporary Research in School Belonging*. Brill Sense.

Baumeister, R.F. & Leary, M.R. (1995). The need to belong: Desire for interpersonal attachments as a fundamental human motivation. *Psychological Bulletin*, *117*(3), 497–529.

Catalano, R.F., Haggerty, K.P., Oesterle, S., Fleming, C.B. & Hawkins, J.D. (2004). The importance of bonding to school for healthy development: Findings from the Social Development Research Group. *Journal of School Health*, *74*(7), 252–261.

Dobia, B., Parada, R., Roffey, S. & Smith, M. (2019). Social and emotional learning: from individual skills to group cohesion. *Educational and Child Psychology*, *36*(2), 79–90.

Dowling, E. & Elliott, D. (2012). *Understanding Children's Needs when Parents Separate*. Speechmark.

Eisenberger, N.I., Lieberman, M.D. & Williams, K.D. (2003). Does rejection hurt? An fMRI study of social exclusion. *Science*, *302*, 290–292.

Lindsay, S. & McPherson, A.C. (2012). Strategies for improving disability awareness and social inclusion of children and young people with cerebral palsy. *Child, Care and Development*, *38*(6), 809–816.

McDonald, B., Lester, K. J., & Michelson, D. (2023). 'She didn't know how to go back': School attendance problems in the context of the COVID-19 pandemic—A multiple stakeholder qualitative study with parents and professionals. *British Journal of Educational Psychology*, *93*, 386–401.

Roffey, S. (2011). Enhancing connectedness in Australian children and young people. *Asian Journal of School Counselling*, *18*(1 & 2), 15–39.

Roffey, S. (2013). Inclusive and Exclusive Belonging: The impact on individual and community wellbeing. *Educational and Child Psychology*, *30*(1), 38–49.

Roffey, S., Boyle, C. & Allen, K-A. (2019). School belonging – Why are our students longing to belong to school? *Educational and Child Psychology*, *36*(2), 5–8.

Rowe, F., Stewart, D. & Patterson, C. (2007). Promoting school connectedness through whole school approaches. *Health Education*, *107*(6), 524–542.

Solomon, D., Watson, M., Battistich, V., Schaps, E. & Delucchi, K. (1996). Creating classrooms that students experience as communities. *American Journal of Community Psychology*, *24*(6), 719–748.

Thorsborne, M. & Blood, P. (2014). *Implementing Restorative Practices in Schools: A Practical Guide to Transforming School Communities*.

Weir, K. (2012). The pain of social rejection. *Science Watch*, *43*(4). American Psychological Society.

Werner, E.E., & Smith, R.S. (2001). *Journeys from Childhood to Midlife: Risk, Resilience, and Recovery*. Cornell University Press.

Wilson, D. (2004). The interface of school climate and school connectedness and relationships with aggression and victimization. *Journal of School Health*, *74*(7), 293–299.

Resources

Books for early years

Mem Fox and Helen Oxenbury (2011). *Ten Little Fingers, Ten Little Toes*. Walker Books.
Julia Donaldson and Axel Schleffer (2020). *The Smeds and the Smoos*.
June and Amy Bates (2023). *The Big Umbrella*. Paula Wiseman Books.

Books for primary 5–7

Molly Potter. *The Same but Different: A Let's Talk Picture Book to Help Young Children Understand Diversity*. Bloomsbury Education.

Books for primary 7–11

Catherine Stephenson. *The Kids Book of Diversity: Empathy, Kindness and Respect for Differences*. Wooden House Books.

Other resources

Restorative Approaches in Schools in the UK https://www.educ.cam.ac.uk/research/programmes/restorativeapproaches/RA-in-the-UK.pdf
Roots of Empathy https://www.rootsofempathy.org/
Roots of Empathy in the UK: https://www.eyalliance.org.uk/roots-empathy-uk
The Babies Teaching Kindness in Class: BBC News https://www.youtube.com/watch?v=TH5mmBEMavI&t=58s
Marg Thorsbourne's TEDx talk about restorative approaches and the power of dialogue https://www.youtube.com/watch?v=9z6mUNk1N9E
Molly Wright's TED Talk *How to Thrive by Five.* https://www.ted.com/talks/molly_wright_how_every_child_can_thrive_by_five
World Café https://www.theworldcafe.com/teachingexpertise.com/articles/developing-effective-participators-using-the-world-cafe/

Resources for SEL

Twinkl has a list of many cards to start conversations categorised by age https://www.twinkl.co.uk/resource/t-l-879-spark-a-conversation-prompt-cards

5 Respect

For individuals, communities and human rights

What do we mean by Respect?

When people are asked to list the qualities of a healthy relationship, Respect frequently comes top of the list. Alongside excellence, it is often referred to in a school's mission statement. But like so many good concepts, this principle may stay in the abstract, not always actioned at either the individual or systemic levels, although sometimes there is insistence on Respect for some – especially those in authority.

Universal Respect is treating others as you would wish to be treated – with consideration, kindness and empathy, focusing on individual dignity and our shared humanity. Barack Obama writes about this Golden Rule in his 2006 book, *The Audacity of Hope*:

> The Golden Rule is not simply a call to sympathy or charity but something more demanding, a call to stand in someone else's shoes and see through their eyes. After all, if (others) are like us, then their struggles are our own. If we fail to help, we diminish ourselves. No-one is exempt from the call to find common ground.

This principle is explicit in nearly every major religion in the world. Here are a few of them:

- Islam: *No one of you is a believer until you desire for your neighbour that which you desire for yourself.*
- Christianity: *Whatever you wish that others do to you, do so to them.*
- Judaism: *What is hateful to you do not do to your neighbour, that is the basic law, all the rest is commentary.*
- Sikhism: *Do as you desire goodness for yourself as you cannot expect tasty fruits if you sow thorny trees.*
- Hinduism: *This is the essence of morality, do not do to others that which if done to you would cause you pain.*
- Shinto: *The heart of the person before you is a mirror. See there your own form.*

Although Respect is aligned with all the other principles in this book, the two closest are Inclusion and Equity. When power and privilege for some dominate, Respect for others often diminishes. People are treated as disposable, not valuable, as numbers not salient beings. They cease to matter in their own right, only in terms of what they can deliver or produce.

This chapter explores what Respect looks like and sounds like in practice – for pupils, teachers, schools, families and communities and the difference that it makes when this principle is in place – and when it isn't.

DOI: 10.4324/9781003428237-6

Respect for children

Respect means valuing the whole person. Every child is both complex and wonderfully unique. There is a risk that we underestimate children because we do not tune into their full potential in all the dimensions of their development and learning. These dimensions include cognitive, social, emotional, psychological, language, spiritual, creative and physical. Teachers who work in target-driven schools may only Respect aspects of individuals that tick academic boxes. When someone is tempted to think, 'This child will never learn', they might consider all the things they have already learnt – like walking, talking, singing, watching, imagining, smiling, creating, choosing. Paying close attention to a toddler over a few weeks can be astonishing. It is like watching a flower unfold as one new skill follows another. You can almost see the millions of new synapses in their brain firing! If that child is in a supportive family, this will be matched by joy as they begin new skills, stumble, practice and finally succeed. This development does not stop when they are 5 years old, but the satisfaction and excitement might, unless that child is in an environment where each step of learning in every domain is respected and celebrated.

Respect for educators

Teaching used to be a profession that was held in high regard. This is still the case in many countries. In Finland, for instance, every teacher has a master's degree and the education system is based on trust rather than external controls, so teachers have high levels of autonomy. They work within an ethical code based on the principles of dignity, truthfulness, fairness, responsibility and freedom (cited in Tirri & Kuusisto, 2022):

- Dignity means Respect for humanity. Teachers are expected to Respect every person, regardless of their gender, sexual orientation, appearance, age, religion, social standing, origin, opinions, abilities and achievements.
- Honesty with oneself and with others, alongside mutual Respect in all communication, is a basic aspect of teachers' work. When helping learners navigate life and their environment, they need to be guided by the truth.
- Fairness is important both when encountering individual learners and groups but also in the work community. Fairness involves, in particular, promoting equality and non-discrimination and avoiding favourites.

Finland is acknowledged as having one of the best education systems in the world, with consistently high rankings in the Organisation for Economic Cooperation and Development (OECD) countries and the highest rate of school completion anywhere.

Although many individual teachers are valued members of their communities, Respect for teachers as a body has been undermined in the UK and elsewhere. High-stakes testing has led to teachers focusing primarily on academic results within a narrow curriculum, as it is this on which they are judged. Even though positive interactions may make all the difference to a child's belief in themselves and overall wellbeing, this is rarely acknowledged as a significant part of the role of an educator.

Respect for diverse communities

An inclusive school culture is one where students and their families feel comfortable being themselves, and not subject to disrespect and discrimination. Students have an identity based in the communities they come from. In a school this may include several different ethnic, racial or religious groups. When a community is accepted without prejudice or judgment, children are able to be proud of who they are and where they come from and more likely to also feel connected to school. It promotes mutual understanding when the curriculum addresses issues that are relevant to diverse cultures. Students learning about each other broadens their knowledge base and gives them insights into alternative ways of thinking and being. Respect is also encapsulated in asking community members what is important to them and listening carefully to the answers.

There is more on this in the chapter on Inclusion.

Self-respect

Treating others respectfully depends to some extent on self-respect. This is different from self-esteem, which is about how you feel about yourself. As can be seen from toxic leadership, it is possible to have high self-esteem and still put others down. Self-respect is the basis of integrity. It is when you know what your human values are and behave in accordance with these. When this happens, you are not unduly upset by criticism or swayed by negative influences. You are confident in who you are, which means you are able to admit mistakes and ask for help. Self-respect enables you to make decisions based on the values you hold rather than what is expedient or will please others.

Why Respect matters

Congruence with the United Nations Convention on the Rights of the Child

Article 2: Respect for the views of the child: Every child has the right to express their views, feelings and wishes in all matters affecting them, and to have their views considered and taken seriously. This right applies at all times, for example during immigration proceedings, housing decisions or the child's day-to-day home life.

Article 28: Discipline in schools must respect children's dignity and their rights.

Article 29: Goals of education: Education must develop every child's personality, talents and abilities to the full. It must encourage the child's respect for human rights, as well as respect for their parents, their own and other cultures, and the environment.

Respect is treating someone with consideration, care and dignity, alongside due regard for their context. It is honouring their presence, listening to what they have to say, and showing interest. It is treating them as an equal and ensuring they have what they need to fully participate. This includes acknowledgement of time and childcare issues. Someone who is respected will be more likely to show Respect to others. Being singled out for criticism, or being lectured, never makes anyone feel good about either themselves or the person being disrespectful.

Respect fosters collaboration to reach mutually agreed goals. It promotes a culture of trust and high social capital. Disrespectful behaviours build toxic environments which foster a spiral of unhealthy relationships.

Respect in practice in the early years

Attachment is critical for healthy child development (Gerhardt, 2015). Babies cry from birth in order to get their physical needs met – for food, comfort or sleep. But smiling as early as 6 weeks is no accident, it is about survival. Infants need their parents/carers to smile back and engage with them in a social dance that promotes their psychological development and wellbeing. Smiling is also very rewarding to new parents and can make up for the exhaustion of looking after a tiny human at all times of the day and night.

This 'serve and return' interaction with significant people needs to continue as the child grows; it is the essence of Respect – it shows they are noticed, valued and matter. It builds trust and a positive sense of self. Without it, children can become insecure, anxious and lack confidence.

Courtesy

Although indicative of Respect, courtesy and good manners sometimes seem to be considered old-fashioned and unnecessary. These micro-interactions, however, make a difference to the quality of relationships. Children are likely to develop these behaviours themselves when they have been modelled to them from a young age. They include the following:

- Asking rather than demanding
- Adding *'please'* when asking for something
- Saying *thank you* when something is given or someone goes out of their way to help
- Saying *no thank you* when declining something
- Checking if someone needs help before taking over
- Not pushing in and saying *'excuse me'* if you want to pass by someone in a tight space
- Saying *sorry* if you have bumped into someone or done something else by accident
- Listening to others without speaking over them
- Waiting your turn
- Asking for things to be shared instead of snatching
- Asking if you need to borrow something and then remembering to return it.

Much of this takes practice and constant reminders – but if this is embedded in an early years culture they will eventually become second nature to oil the wheels of relationships.

Cultural awareness

Cultural awareness that promotes Respect for diversity can be introduced from an early age. This both promotes connection and helps to inhibit bullying later on. There are many books to support this, as well as cartoons with characters from different backgrounds. Everyone enjoys music, and children can be introduced to a wide range of instruments that are played all over the world. Cooking foods for different cultural ceremonies also broadens perspectives.

Children may have heard racist or sexist comments at home or in their neighbourhood and repeat these in an early years or primary school setting. It does not help to assume that children hold these views themselves, so any response needs to be measured rather than condemnatory. Even saying things like 'that's not a nice thing to say about someone' can backfire if children have heard this from a parent. Perhaps ask children to explain what they mean. They may have no idea that they are using words/labels that are derogatory. Briefly explain why this language is not used in this school. Ask them how they would feel if people spoke about them in a similar way. Suppose they have blue eyes and other people were spreading it around that everyone with blue eyes was not the sort of person you would want to sit next to. Would that be right? Say that we Respect everyone here because every single person matters – and this means being kind about what we say, as well as what we do. If this continues, it may be a good idea to address it with groups of children.

The same applies to children who are used to people swearing at home and freely use this language in the early years setting. The best way to address this is by repeating the message that this is not how we speak to each other here and giving children alternative ways to express themselves.

Respect in practice in the primary classroom

Teaching and learning

John Hattie, in his meta-analysis of effective education (2008), talks about having Respect for students and their ideas. He says that it is not the extent of teacher subject knowledge that raises attainment but knowing how to introduce new content in a way that integrates this with students' prior knowledge. He concludes that teachers need to talk less and listen more! Listening allows the teacher to learn about the students' prior achievements and understanding. Listening demonstrates Respect by showing interest, finding out important information and promoting more effective dialogue. It models reciprocity and Respect for the students' perspectives. By listening, teachers model deep communication skills more than just the transmission of knowledge.

Teacher-student relationships

When a child's efforts to communicate have been met with disinterest, their experiments to 'see what will happen if' have led to disapproval and sometimes punishment, it is harder for them to take risks with their learning. They may be positioned negatively as 'attention-seeking' when it is more likely they are 'attention needing'. Although educators cannot replace the importance of parental bonding, establishing and maintaining positive relationships in the primary school can make a significant difference to a child's self-concept, their willingness to listen and their engagement with learning. Here are some ways to do this:

- Welcome children warmly – by name as soon as possible. One Palestinian teacher has a picture chart by her classroom door, and as children come in they point to the way they want to be greeted – a handshake, hug, high five or fist bump.
- Give bite-sized attention. Find out something not to do with school – such as pets, siblings or teams they follow. Regular Circle Solutions sessions facilitate accessing this knowledge in a safe way. Follow up in brief conversations: "How's your baby sister?" "Your team did well on Saturday".
- Busy teachers don't have much time to listen to pupils, so when opportunities do arise, the listening needs to be active. This means acknowledging what is being said, validating associated feelings and asking for clarification when needed.
- Positive relationships with primary-aged children are less likely to be fostered with bland praise than with specific feedback. A thumbs up for progress, kindness or positive behaviour adds to the child's understanding that they are liked and matter.
- Children who already have a low sense of self find criticism hard to take. It is easier for them if the ratio of positive to negative comments is about five to one, e.g. "I like the way you …" or "I have noticed that …"
- A child who is reprimanded for their behaviour may take this as a signal that they are not liked themselves. Adults need to make it clear that it is the behaviour that is unacceptable, not the child. A respectful response says something positive first, such as, "You can be so kind sometimes, but this behaviour is not acceptable".
- When settling down to work is an issue, first remind the child what they are expected to do and ask them to tell you the first thing they are going to do. Then walk away rather than stand over them.

Rudeness and disrespect

Some pupils model their behaviour on negative experiences at home. Others may react with abusive language to a threat to their sense of self in some way – perhaps being asked to do a piece of work that they do not believe they have the knowledge or skills for. Respect for teachers, however, does not lie in compliance or even politeness. Teachers have choices in this situation, even though their emotional response may trigger some knee-jerk reactions. Going on the defensive and arguing with a student is never a successful strategy and often fuels the situation, making things worse. Saying, *"You can't talk to me like that"*, is unlikely to be effective either.

Maintaining self-respect means not taking this behaviour personally and staying calm. Easier said than done, but a supportive and emotionally literate school culture that recognises why pupils behave the way they do will help. Modelling courtesy is also useful.

If you have built a positive relationship with this pupil, one or more of the following responses may reduce the tension in this situation:

- *This is unacceptable. I treat you with Respect, and I expect the same from you.*
- *Take a break and come back and talk to me when you have calmed down.*
- *Did you mean to be rude to me, or are you just upset?* (Sometimes students can be surprised by how their behaviour is interpreted.)
- *That might be OK when you are talking with friends but not with me now.*
- *How else might you say this so I can hear you properly?*

Sometimes rudeness can be the last straw in a difficult day. Rather than react at the time, you might say, "I am finding your behaviour disrespectful and distressing, so I am going to walk away now and talk to you later about this". This also models good practice.

Respect in practice across the primary school

Respectful leadership

Despite beliefs that autocratic practices focused on achieving targets are what is needed in schools, there is now a considerable body of research on effective leadership that indicates that it is the soft skills that empower and motivate staff, leading to better learning and well-being outcomes for all.

Scott (2003) ranked the qualities of effective school leaders as:

1 Emotional intelligence. This includes staying calm, keeping things in perspective and maintaining a sense of humour.
2 Social intelligence, including dealing effectively with conflict situations, being able to empathise and work productively with people from a wide range of backgrounds, respecting and honouring diversity, a willingness to listen to different points of view before making decisions, and contributing positively to team projects.
3 Intellectual abilities, including identifying priorities and being flexible. Generic and specific skills covered having a clear justified vision for the school and being able to organise and manage time effectively.

Whether they are public or private, formal or informal, it is the everyday conversations that make the difference to levels of trust and Respect, and critically how people feel in the workplace. Positive organisational psychologists Dutton & Spreitzer (2014) refer to high-quality connections as those that:

- listen attentively to what people have to say,
- are constructively responsive,
- make requests rather than demands,
- are task enabling,
- show trust by relying on others to meet their commitments,
- encourage playfulness.

Although the minutiae of interactions can build either high social capital or a toxic environment, policies embedded in Respect make a difference to expectations and outcomes. School leaders are instrumental in this, as illustrated in the Families First case study.

Families First

As a Headteacher, my job is to look after the staff, so that they can look after the children. When staff experience personal challenges such as divorce, sickness, bereavement or other family issues that are clearly affecting their work, we head for the Staff Wellbeing Policy, rather than threatening them with sanctions. We consider how we can hold people through their challenges, keeping the long-term goal of their personal thriving at heart. This includes prioritising time for the staff member and creating safe spaces for them to feel seen and heard without judgment.

Within this space, trust is built for staff to be honest about how they are feeling and any negative impact on their work. We then explore solutions together. These may include additional class support, more PPA time (Preparation, Planning and Assessment), facilitating a reduction of hours or a block of paid leave. Sometimes holding a space for personal reflection is enough. There may be a short-term cost, but over time, individual stories create a staff team who collectively know they are held in unconditional love when life gets tough and consequently go above and beyond for the children once they are back on track. Treating staff with respect and care means that they stay in our school and our profession.

Tina Farr, Headteacher, St. Ebbe's Primary School, Oxford

Transformational leaders able to 'turn schools around' are emotionally literate and put a high value on positive relationships. The sustainability of change depends on the level of trust that permeates a school. Bryk and Schneider (2002) identified this as Respect, competence, personal regard for others and integrity. High levels of trust between adults in a school predict higher student academic outcomes.

Respect for teachers

Although pay is one reason for teacher attrition, it is not the only one. Teachers routinely cite stress, overload, working conditions, lack of support from leadership, dealing with challenging pupil behaviour, little autonomy and not feeling valued. It is the accumulation of issues over time, eventually triggered by something specific, that prompts a teacher to walk away (DfE, 2018). For education systems to function well, educators need to be respected for their knowledge, professionalism and effort. Educators, like students, are multidimensional beings and not simply cogs in a machine. For children to flourish, we must cherish their teachers. The following example is just one way of doing this.

Children who have experienced trauma do not leave their experiences behind when in class. Teachers may find themselves facing the challenges these pupils present on a daily basis. This is not simply a question of 'discipline' but a complex and overwhelming emotional load. Respect for teachers does not lie in student compliance but in a support system which helps them navigate these challenges.

Respect for teachers and the role of supervision

My own experience, and those of the teachers in my research, includes having had children in their classrooms who have experienced trauma. These pupils exhibit dysregulated, challenging behaviour as well as high levels of complex emotional need. Unsurprisingly this takes a serious toll on teacher wellbeing (Cole, 2010). Research indicates how psychologically demanding it is to contain other people's trauma (McCann & Pearlman, 1990), but unlike other professionals such as social workers or psychologists, classroom teachers in the UK do not have regular formal support to manage their emotional response to these situations. To both reduce teacher burnout and promote positive pupil outcomes, this needs to change.

Teachers recognise that for pupils with a history of adverse experience, the classroom environment can be overwhelming, and although they often strive to respond with empathy and understanding, this has an emotional impact on them. For teachers to be effective in forming strong relationships with pupils that promote learning and positive behaviour, they need to be emotionally nurtured themselves (Rae, 2012). Alongside a school environment that offers emotional and physical safety to all members of its community, a supportive, trauma-informed supervision framework is crucial to retaining and motivating classroom teachers and affording them the psychological safety and respect they deserve.

(Adapted from the thesis: **Using hermeneutic phenomenology and visual representation to explore trauma in the primary classroom: the case for classroom teachers to access supervision,** *by Sam McNally, 2022).*

Mutual Respect between home and school

Even though the wellbeing and learning of children is optimally a joint enterprise between home and school, this is not always played out in practice, as parents blame schools when things for their child do not go well, and schools can easily look to parents/carers when children do not comply with learning or behavioural expectations. Mutual Respect can be hard to develop and even more challenging to maintain.

When children are first registered at a school, welcoming parents as their child's first and most important teachers both honours and respects this role and establishes an understanding of joint responsibility. Acknowledging that parents are the 'experts' on their child may also offer a raised appreciation of their own knowledge and possibly also promote a deeper interest, asking questions such as, *"What is your child's favourite toy at the moment?" "What helps to soothe your child when they are upset?" "What can your child do all by themselves?" "Who in the family has the best relationship with them?"*

It is useful to clearly communicate the school's priorities. If the wellbeing of the whole child is as important as their learning, setting this out early and often, and explaining why, may help to defer potential conflicts. Also, clarifying when teachers are available for a conversation and when they are not can reduce stress for staff of trying to be everything to everyone. It makes sense to link this to Respect for children's learning.

Families are not homogenous and may not conform to the traditional nuclear unit. There may be a single parent looking after a child, or two parents of the same sex – maybe even co-parenting with a third adult. Other carers may be significant. In Aboriginal communities, for instance, grandparents often raise the children – and in traditional indigenous culture every woman accepts mothering responsibilities with the children in the community.

It is easy to jump to conclusions about families when children's learning, development and especially behaviour is not what is expected or wanted in school. Parents, often mothers, can easily be negatively positioned as uncaring. A more respectful starting point is to assume that parents usually want the best for their children and do the best they can with the skills, knowledge, support and resources available to them – this includes emotional resources.

Parents who are demanding and appear aggressive may feel they have to 'fight' for their child. Their experience with authority may so far have left them feeling angry and helpless, and a teacher may be seen as just another authority figure. Acknowledging their parental role as protector and defender makes for a better beginning to a conversation than confrontation. It is then worth saying something positive and caring about their child, showing that you too have their best interests at heart. Schools are restricted by policies and resources and unlikely to be able to agree with everything parents want, but by respecting their right to ask, listening to their views and explaining what is and is not possible, it may be possible to reach agreements. Monitoring outcomes matters, so ongoing communication at a level that works for everyone is valuable, perhaps a weekly phone call until the end of term or, even better, an occasional text saying what has been achieved in either learning or behaviour.

See the chapter on Safety for what to do if a parent comes into school under the influence of drugs or alcohol, aggressive or verbally abusive.

Respectful meetings

Meetings are often where the minutiae of respectful interactions are demonstrated – or not. Sometimes those calling the meeting have an agenda where they want to achieve certain outcomes and give lip service to consultation. Respect, however, is encapsulated in maximising participation, so that everyone feels they have been heard and their views matter. When this happens, the decisions made are more likely to be enacted. When people leave a meeting feeling sidelined, there is little motivation to cooperate. The following outlines good practice.

Information

Make the purpose of the meeting clear to everyone and ensure that all participants have the information they need beforehand rather than being given papers as they arrive. Ensure that families can access this information. Not everyone can read or speak the language of the school. Spell out any acronyms and explain what words mean where necessary. There is an educators' vocabulary, and it is easy to make assumptions that people understand what terms like 'curriculum' or 'pedagogy' mean. When I first went to New South Wales, people talked about ISTB's; I had no idea what this meant, and it took a while to summon up the courage to ask and find that it stood for 'Itinerant Support Teacher for Behaviour'. And I then had to look up 'itinerant' to discover it means travelling from place to place!

Invitation

When inviting families for meetings about an individual pupil for whom there is concern, check out when would be a good time for them and invite them as experts on their child. Suggest they bring a friend or other family member. This person is not only there for support at the time but also for talking things over afterwards. Discussing a child's difficulties can be emotional, and people may miss information if they are feeling overwhelmed.

The room

Sometimes families need to bring a young child with them. Having some toys and books available shows you have considered their needs. Setting chairs in a circle means everyone can see and hopefully hear each other and puts everyone on the same level.

Chairing

Suggest that each person introduces themselves, including their role. If staff are called by their first name, that option needs to be given to everyone. The chairperson sets the tone of the meeting, and it helps to begin by saying something positive about the student. Their role is also to make sure that the important issues are discussed and that everyone has the opportunity to contribute. This may mean both listening respectfully and gently reminding the more dominant voices that others also need to have their say. Keeping the discussion solution-focused rather than dissecting problems is not always easy but is a much better use of people's valuable time. Give time for questions and clarification.

Timings

It helps to be clear about when a meeting will start and when it will end – and stick to these timings. This is being considerate of other commitments people may have. Both families and teachers will be distracted and lose focus if the meeting goes over time.

Interruptions

Ask everyone to switch phones off or to silent. And minimise potential interruptions. These give the impression that other things are more important than the meeting taking place.

Recording

Ask everyone if it is OK to record the main points in writing so everyone can have feedback about what was decided.

At the end

Ten to 15 minutes before the end of the meeting, the chairperson summarises the main points that have been discussed, especially any agreed actions. Check if anyone wants to add anything, set a review date if appropriate and then thank everyone for coming.

Rights Respecting Schools

It is valuable for children to know what their rights are as described in the United Nations Convention on the Rights of the Child, as this also gives them an understanding of their responsibilities in standing up for their own rights and those of others. The four guiding principles are:

- Non-discrimination (Article 2)
- Best interest of the child (Article 3)
- Right to life survival and development (Article 6)
- Right to be heard (Article 12).

The Rights Respecting Schools Award is a UNICEF initiative. The organisation works with schools to put children's rights at the centre of policy and practice in the school and create safe and inspiring places to learn, where children are respected, their talents are nurtured and they are able to thrive. These four standards contribute towards this:

1 *Rights-respecting values underpin leadership and management*
   The best interests of the child are a top priority in all actions. Leaders are committed to placing the values and principles of the UN Convention on the Rights of the Child (UNCROC) at the heart of all policies and practice.
2 *The whole school community learns about UNCROC*
   The Convention is made known to children and adults. Young people and adults use this shared understanding to work for global justice and sustainable living.
3 *The school has a rights-respecting ethos*
   Young people and adults collaborate to develop and maintain a rights-respecting school community, based on UNCROC, in all areas and in all aspects of school life.
4 *Children and young people are empowered to become active citizens and learners*
   Every child has the right to say what they think in all matters affecting them and to have their views taken seriously. Young people develop the confidence, through their experience of an inclusive rights-respecting school community, to play an active role in their own learning and to speak and act for the rights of all to be respected locally and globally.

A Rights Respecting School

From the first moment you enter Glade, you feel a sense of purpose and well-being. Respect permeates our school ethos and workplace, ensuring everyone feels valued and welcome.

Achieving our 'Rights Respecting Gold Award' for the second time running shows that the principles of the United Nations Convention on the Rights of the Child (UNCROC) are fully embedded into our ideology, culture and curriculum.

Diversity and inclusion threads through all areas of our curriculum. Children are represented in books, poetry, authors and artists that they study: this contributes to well-being (one of our core curriculum drivers). They understand that respect means that you accept others for who they are, even when they are 'different' from you or you don't agree with them.

Our 'Well-being Award' is evidence that mental health and well-being sit at the heart of school life at Glade. To further establish our reputation as a rights respecting school, we are now working on achieving the Anti-Racist Schools Award.

The duty-bearers (adults) at school use restorative language to allow children to understand the impact of their behaviours, maintaining their respect and dignity at all times. Rights and values are promoted in class discussions and weekly assemblies. Children also campaign for issues related to their rights and that of their peers (recycling and clean air are some examples).

Children comment that the rights are now engrained in them, making it easy to implement respectful attitudes towards all they meet and work with.

Farzana Hussain: Headteacher; Sumana Jain: Deputy Headteacher, Glade Primary School, Ilford, UK

The impact of Rights Respecting Schools appears to be far-reaching (UNICEF, 2016). An evaluation of over 500 schools in England, Wales, Scotland and Northern Ireland indicated that between 93% and 98% of headteachers considered that being a Rights Respecting

School enhanced pupil Respect for themselves and others, improved relationships and behaviour, saw young people more engaged with learning and led to more positive attitudes towards diversity. 76% reported a decrease in bullying and exclusions.

Respect for diverse communities

It is easy to jump to conclusions about other people based on limited information and stereotypes. How people dress and speak, their marital status, home circumstances, religion and profession can quickly lead to assumptions about expectations, motivations, intentions, values and possibilities. Communication and actions can then be based on misinformation, which can create unnecessary difficulties rather than opening up options for resolving issues. One parent was told by a teacher that she thought her son had problems in school because she was a single mother. The only way to avoid this sort of disrespect is to resist making judgments, and instead ask questions to ascertain useful information.

Respect for diverse cultures is demonstrated in what is seen and heard around a school. When some of the staff in a school also come from the communities the school serves, this also gives positive messages about the value of that community.

Signs and communications need to be in community languages and interpreters available when needed.

Behaviour

The language of disorders and a respectful alternative

There used to be schools in the UK for 'maladjusted children'. Those students were not 'maladjusted' – they were adjusting to the circumstances and experiences that had shaped them. The label of 'maladjusted' placed the problem squarely within them and indicated that they were the ones who had to change. This is also true of many psychiatric 'disorders'. The *Diagnostic and Statistics Manual, Fifth Edition (DSM-5)* lists at least 157, some of which are simply descriptions of behaviours for which there is little biological/chemical basis. There is considerable controversy about this deficit psychiatric approach, but when young children are given psychotropic drugs so they can sit still in the classroom, something is not right.

The British Psychological Society has developed an alternative framework for exploring a child's difficulties. Instead of looking at what is 'wrong', with someone, it asks, "What has happened to them?" "What impact has this had?" This is called the Power, Threat, Meaning Framework, and can be accessed from the links in the resources.

Sometimes it is hard, if not impossible, to know what has been happening in a child's life. It is unlikely anyone will be aware of the impact of postnatal depression on the development of emotional regulation in a 4-year-old, or that the disappearance of a significant person underlies confusion and rejection in a 7-year-old or that witnessing family violence is traumatising for a 10-year-old. Few in a school have the time to find out such history or circumstances, but it makes sense to begin with the premise that a child who is acting out or whose behaviour is otherwise unacceptable has a reason for this and is hurting in some way. Pupils need to know what is and is not acceptable in the classroom and not be a danger to themselves or others, but otherwise it makes sense to treat every child with care and Respect. There are many biographies where individuals who have made a success of their lives despite challenging circumstances and defiant behaviour in school attribute this to the support of a teacher who treated them with kindness. Teachers make more difference than they know.

Respect and social and emotional learning (SEL)

Respect in Circle Solutions is summarised by 'we listen to each other'. This means that when it is one person's turn to speak, often signalled by holding the 'talking stick', others do not interrupt or speak amongst themselves. If that happens the facilitator stops everything and waits until the talking stops. They may use a 'proximal praise' strategy by thanking the person nearest the talkers for waiting quietly. Respect is also activated by the 'no put downs' guideline. Participants may say 'personal positives' to each other, but statements that demean someone are not acceptable. This extends to verbal expressions – raising your eyebrows at what someone has said is a 'put down'.

Activities in SEL

The following activity enables students to understand the concept of Respect more fully.

Strengths in Circles Cards:

The Strengths in Circles Cards have seven statements on Respect for students to discuss in small groups. The ones most suitable for primary-aged children are:

* We listen to each other.
* We hear each other's stories.
* We show interest in each other.
* We do not put anyone down.

Children are in random groups of three or four: for each phrase, they are asked to discuss:

– What does this mean?
– Is this good to have in our class?
– Why is it a good thing?
– Is it already happening?
– How would we know?
– Is there anything we could do to have more of this?

It is not necessary for all these questions to be given at the same time. When they take place over successive Circle sessions, this gives pupils opportunities to identify and think about what is happening in their class and how it makes them feel.

Trust

Trust is an aspect of Respect, and similar activities can help children understand what it means in practice, as we can see from the following examples:

If Trust came into this classroom today, what would we notice? What would we see and hear? What would people be feeling? What might someone feel when Trust isn't there?
In pairs, talk about and then finish these sentences:

– Trust is when …
– Being able to trust someone means …
– We can be trustworthy by …

Hypotheticals:

Small groups talk about these situations and decide what would be a respectful thing to do and why.

1 A family comes into a bus. There are two children aged about 5 and 8, and a mother who is carrying a baby. The two children run to sit on the only seat available.
2 A dad and his son are in the queue for the cinema. While they are waiting, the son asks for popcorn. His dad gets him some, and the boy grabs handfuls to eat. He drops bits of sticky popcorn all over the floor.
3 A homeless person is in a doorway, covered by a blanket. Two teenagers come past and take a pack of sandwiches that someone has left for the homeless person.
4 A new member of staff walks with a limp. Some pupils follow him up the corridor, mimicking his walk and laughing.

Whole Circle:

Children stand in a circle, and the teacher says something that you are either born with or not. If it's something you were born with, you jump into the circle; if not, you jump back. Skin colour, being able to read, having blue eyes, being able to climb, having a sister, helping at home, having ten fingers, being able to sleep, having a belly button. The aim is to show that some things cannot change while others are learnt or developed.

Respect checklist

	This is in place – we know it is effective because ...	*Working on it – our actions to date are ...*	*Just started – our next step will be ...*
All staff have discussed and defined Respect and self-respect			
Respect is modelled in all interactions			
Courtesy is modelled and encouraged			
Staff are skilled in active listening			
There is a 'no put downs' policy across the school			
Meetings are respectful			
People trust each other			
The school is 'Rights Respecting'			
Behaviour is seen as communication			
Pupils have been learning about Respect in SEL			

Respect in the future

Every day we hear of behaviour that demeans others, often from people who are in positions of authority and who are employed to take care of the welfare of others. Those being abused or denigrated are invariably vulnerable in some way – asylum seekers, mentally ill, children, ethnic minorities, the elderly and women, especially when alone.

If we are to build a society where Respect for others is part of the fabric of daily life, then every child should experience Respect at school and learn what it means from the day they enter until the day they leave. A one-off lesson in respectful relationships is better than nothing but nowhere near enough. Respect needs to be threaded through the learning environment.

Although it is a minority who behave this way, there is continuing reluctance in calling them out. Respect is also due to those who are prepared to put themselves on the line as opponents of this behaviour.

References, further reading and resources

Bryk, A. & Schneider, B. (2002). *Trust in Schools*. Russell Sage.

Cole, T. (2010). Ease practitioner stress to improve services for children and young people with SEBD. *Emotional and Behavioural Difficulties, 15*(1), 1–4.

Department for Education (2018). *Factors Affecting Teacher Retention. Qualitative Investigation. Research Report*. Cooper Gibson Research.

Dutton, J.E. & Spreitzer, G.M. (Eds) (2014). *How to be a Positive Leader: Small Actions, Big Impact*. Berrett-Koehler Publishers

Hattie, J. (2008). *Visible Learning: A Meta-analysis of Over 800 Meta-analyses Relating to Achievement*. Routledge.

Gerhardt, S. (2015). *Why Love Matters: How Affection Shapes a Baby's Brain*. 2nd Edition. Routledge.

McCann, I.L. & Pearlman, L.A. (1990). Vicarious traumatization: A framework for understanding the psychological effects of working with victims. *Journal of Traumatic Stress, 3*, 131–149.

McNally, S. (2022). *Using hermeneutic phenomenology and visual representation to explore trauma in the primary classroom: the case for classroom teachers to access supervision*. Unpublished.

Obama, B. (2006). *The Audacity of Hope*. Crown/Three Rivers Press.

Rae, T. (2012). Developing emotional literacy approaches for staff and students. Developing an approach in an SEBD school. In J. Visser, H. Daniels, T. Cole & C. Forlin (Eds) *Transforming Troubled Lives: Strategies and Interventions for Children with Social, Emotional, and Behavioural Difficulties. International Perspectives*. Emerald.

Scott, G. (2003). *Learning Principals - Leadership Capability & Learning*. University of Technology, Sydney. Commissioned Research for NSW DET., March, 2003.

Tirri, K. & Kuusisto, E. (2022). *Teachers' Professional Ethics: Theoretical Frameworks and Empirical Research from Finland*. Brill.

UNICEF. (2016). *Research on Rights Respecting Schools*. https://www.unicef.org.uk/rights-respecting-schools/the-rrsa/impact-of-rrsa/evidence_2016/

Other sources and further reading

Johnson, L. & Boyle, M. (2020). *A Straight Talking Introduction to The Power Threat Meaning Framework: An Alternative to Psychiatric Diagnosis*. PCCS Books.

Roffey, S. (2002). *Schools Behaviour and Families: Frameworks for Working Together*. Routledge.

Roffey. S. (2005). *Respect in Practice – the challenge of emotional literacy in education. Conference paper ROF05356*. Australian Educational Research.

Roffey, S. (2007). Transformation and emotional literacy: the role of school leaders in developing a caring community. *Leading and Managing, 13*(1), 16–30.

Roffey, S. (2012). Pupil wellbeing: Teacher wellbeing: Two sides of the same coin? *Educational and Child Psychology, 29*(4), 8–17.

Roffey, S. & Parry, J. (2013). *Special Needs in the Early Years: Promoting Collaboration, Communication and Co-ordination*. 3rd edition. Routledge.

Resources

British Psychological Society: *Power, Threat, Meaning Framework*: https://www.bps.org.uk/member-networks/division-clinical-psychology/power-threat-meaning-framework

Equality and Human Rights Commission: This report shows how schools have implemented Human Rights Education across England, Scotland and Wales: https://www.equalityhumanrights.com/en/publication-download/exploring-human-rights-education-great-britain

UNICEF: The Rights Respecting School Award: https://www.unicef.org.uk/rights-respecting-schools/the-rrsa/

TEDx Talk by Sue Roffey: *School as Family*: https://www.youtube.com/watch?v=XaHOQ9DmffE

6 Equity
Fairness and flexibility

What do we mean by Equity?

Equality has benefits for both individuals and society. The least gap between the privileged and the poor in any country promotes higher levels of wellbeing. But for all children to do well in education, we must think differently from the 'one-size-fits-all' approach, as this clearly does not work for everyone. For children to have equal opportunities to flourish and learn, we need both education policy and schools to be adaptable, flexible and fair. This is the basis of Equity.

There are several ways in which students may be disadvantaged – many of these interact with each other. Most of the time the focus is on poverty, race or geography, but the list here shows that there is no such thing as the average or 'normal' child and that the factors that influence pupil attainment are many and varied.

Socio-economic factors

The impact of poverty was writ large in the pandemic, when pupils were expected to learn at home. Not all had the technology they needed, and living in cramped accommodation meant they did not have the space to study. Poverty also negatively affects nutrition, warmth, sleep, security, mental health and relationships. When children have such challenges at home, school can become a lifeline with the provision of basic needs, access to the internet and after-school activities.

Social factors

Inequity is associated with discrimination, where there are prejudiced expectations of certain groups related to race, class, language, religion, gender or disability. This is particularly the case for indigenous and migrant communities everywhere. Some subjects still have a gender bias, and in many countries girls are denied equal access to education, an issue that was exacerbated during the pandemic. There is now a wealth of information about adapting educational approaches and the curriculum for specific groups.

Family factors

Some pupils may live in dysfunctional or abusive households, where they get little educational support or encouragement. Some parents may not value education themselves, and even if they do want their children to do well, they do not have the knowledge or resources to support them. In other more economically advantaged homes, some families are so focused on being successful they do not foster the relational environment that children need to thrive.

DOI: 10.4324/9781003428237-7

Being in care

The number of children placed in care in the UK has increased in recent years. Those who are 'looked after' have a range of poor outcomes, including lower educational attainments, poorer physical and mental health, and involvement with juvenile justice. As adults they are more likely to face stark health and socio-economic inequalities in the years and decades after (Sacker et al., 2021).

Loss

Although rarely acknowledged in schools as an impediment to wellbeing and learning, many children struggle, at least temporarily, with the absence of significant people in their lives. Bereavement is usually a more straightforward loss than family breakdown, but for both, how affected the child will be depends on how close they were to the person they have lost. Nearly half of all children in Western countries are living with one parent by the time they are 16, so although family breakdown is a common occurrence, it still has a profound impact on individuals. Depending on prior levels of conflict, how the breakdown has been mediated, and the age of the child, responses can range from relief, confusion, rejection and anger to sadness and fear for the future. Often children will express strong emotions at school rather than at home, and unless teachers take the time to find out what is happening, behavioural problems can escalate. This can also happen when new people come into children's lives.

Disability

Although some children have disabilities that require formal assessment and specified intervention, such as in an Education, Health and Care Plan (UK), many more need adaptations and/or support to fully access the curriculum. This includes hearing loss, poor eyesight, problems with the printed word, sequencing, organisational skills and more.

Cultural and language factors

School systems, values and expectations may be different to the home culture, and this can lead to misunderstandings and a lack of collaboration that disadvantages pupils. Children who are newly arrived may have skills and abilities that are not immediately evident because they are coping with major changes in their lives, learning a new language, trying to fit in and learn 'how things happen' in their new environment. It is best to reserve judgment while this process is underway. Although children invariably learn a second language at school over time, they may need visual and contextual support whilst working towards fluency.

Geographic factors

In some areas, funding cuts to local authorities have meant that schools themselves are disadvantaged, with poor infrastructure, inadequate resources and sometimes a lack of staff. In some of the poorest areas, schools have had to rely on charities to give pupils breakfast before they come to class and have secured warm clothing for them in winter.

Trauma

Children who have experienced either incidental or chronic trauma may not be able to focus and learn. Amongst other things, they may be hypervigilant, sleep-deprived, emotionally volatile and experiencing flashbacks. This takes children to a level of distress that is hard both for them and for those trying to teach them. Trauma-informed positive education in these circumstances can support both pupils and educators.

Equity is probably the most challenging of the positive education principles to implement, but it is also the most important for a future thriving society. Although Equity is largely dependent on the socio-cultural-political macro-level in an ecological model (Bronfenbrenner, 1979), it is worth remembering that all levels interact with each other bidirectionally, and that systems change over time. Here we explore what we can do at every level to give each child the best chance to learn and flourish, despite the circumstances into which they were born or what has happened to them since.

Why does Equity matter?

Congruence with the United Nations Convention on the Rights of the Child

Article 29 (goals of education): Education must develop every child's personality, talents and abilities to the full.

Article 23 (children with a disability): A child with a disability has the right to live a full and decent life with dignity and, as far as possible, independence and to play an active part in the community.

Article 39 (recovery from trauma and re-integration): Children who have experienced neglect, abuse, exploitation or torture or are victims of war must receive special support to help them recover their health, dignity, self-respect and social life.

We all start life in differing circumstances – some are born into privilege or as citizens of a nation that looks after people who have fallen on hard times, while others find themselves in families and communities who have very few resources. Some are born surrounded by love, care and support, others less so.

While there has been a reduction in global inequality over the last few decades, within countries inequalities have increased, especially in advanced economies. This leads to unwanted consequences, not only for the disadvantaged but also for society as a whole.

Reversing cycles of disadvantage

An overwhelming reason for Equity in positive education is intervening in cycles of deprivation. Deprivation, with all the disadvantages and hardships this brings for individuals, families, communities and society, is not an inevitable fact of life. The following are just two major examples of historical successful interventions that reversed cycles of disadvantage, both based in the UK.

The welfare state

After the Second World War in Britain, there was a determined effort to create a country fit for all to live in. The welfare state was established, and millions of people, especially the post-war generation, benefitted from a new National Health Service, free higher education and a social security system to help those in need. The impact was significant. Children from previously impoverished households had opportunities beyond their parents' dreams. Upward social mobility enabled more individuals to hold down good jobs, many being the first in their family to go to university and attain a profession, such as teachers, lawyers and doctors. The post-war generation often earned enough to buy their own homes, were free from fear of poverty and had hope of a brighter future.

The benefits to the nation were immense – but the system was fragile in the face of capitalism and the growing influence of market forces, increasing individualism and an erroneous 'belief in a just world' (Lerner, 1980). This is the basis of 'the American dream', which says that everyone can 'make it' by their own efforts if they work hard enough. If you are not successful, it is deemed to be your fault. This ignores the contexts into which people are born or the life events that might befall them, and risks creating a society lacking in empathy or humanity.

Sure Start

In 1998, with a growing awareness of the vital importance of the early years for life trajectories, the Sure Start program was initiated across the UK. Childcare centres were established to support young families from pregnancy to when children were 4, especially in areas of disadvantage. These provided integrated multi-agency services, including childcare and early education programs, health services, play facilities, parenting classes and specialised family support services. A government evaluation (Gaheer & Paul, 2016) found that overall these provided value for money, although it was not possible to evaluate the longer term and accumulative impact. There were clear indications, however, of Sure Start intervening in the cycle of disadvantage. The development of a more effective home learning environment was associated with several of the services provided, especially when used when babies were between 1 and 3 years. Mothers reported better life satisfaction and less impulse for harsh discipline. Children were physically healthier and had more stimulating and less chaotic home environments. The biggest impact on child health, however, is seen in adolescence. According to research by the Institute of Fiscal Studies (Cattan et al., 2021), around 13,000 admissions of older children to hospital each year were likely prevented by the work of Sure Start children's centres. The evaluation goes on to estimate the positive impact on school attendance and achievement, reduction in crime and antisocial behaviour, reducing smoking and improvements in mental health.

The number of Sure Start children's centres peaked at around 3,620 in 2010, but with the following government's policy of austerity, funding has been reduced by 60%, and many have been closed down or offer reduced services. There is now a resurgence of cross-party interest in establishing family centres with similar functions, but at the moment most initiatives are funded by charities rather than government.

Economic value of early intervention

The Nobel-prize-winning economist James Heckman estimates that there is a 13% return on investment in the early years in terms of better educational, health and social outcomes. The Royal Foundation Centre for Early Childhood in the UK, reporting on research from the London School of Economics (2021), calculated that failing to positively intervene early in children's lives cost England at least £16.13 billion each year from supporting children in care to physical and mental health needs, crime, unemployment and lost productivity. The Times Education Commission Report Bringing Out the Best (Seldon & Sylvester, 2022) notes *"the missing geniuses of this generation whose potential is being wasted by a flawed and unfair education system"* and points out that billions may be lost to the economy as a result.

Community safety

The term 'structural violence' has been used to define unequal distribution of power and resources said to be built into the structure of a society (Galtung, 1969, 1990). It is more deadly than physical violence perpetrated by individuals, as it stealthily but consistently prevents groups of citizens from having their basic needs met. This leads to economic deprivation, injustice, poor mental and physical health and often earlier mortality. The resulting resentment and need to find someone to blame can lead to community unrest, conflict and actual violence. It is unsurprising that those in power will point to sections of the community as a justified target, such as refugees, the homeless or ethnic communities. Actual violence is sometimes referred to as the tip of the iceberg in full view and often in the media spotlight, whereas the rest of the iceberg – out of sight – is the structural and cultural violence that enables it. Nelson Mandela is one of many who recognised that while poverty, injustice, and gross inequality persist in society, no one can 'truly rest'. It follows that policies and practices that promote Equity can boost social cohesion and reduce conflict.

Democracy

We have an education system in many countries that does not adequately prepare young people to be active and engaged citizens in the 21st century. Politicians may rely on voter ignorance or apathy and belief in what they read on social media in order to be elected on platforms that are not always in people's best interests. Economic wellbeing is important but not the only purpose of a good education. Equity as a principle therefore includes citizenship, critical thinking and social justice. Children and young people need to know how their country is run, who makes decisions, what vested interests are, why voting matters and how to differentiate between fact and fiction.

Collaboration

Competition in education has a wide range of negative consequences. When children are measured against each other, there are always going to be winners and losers. This may be fine for those who do well academically, but constant failure is not motivating, and students lose enthusiasm for learning. When education is about enabling children to become the best of themselves, failure is not on the agenda.

When schools themselves are measured against each other, they are less likely to collaborate. Although there is an increasing expectation on schools to support one another to facilitate educational improvement and Equity, the *"English educational system remains a deeply marketised arena in which schools must compete over pupils, funding and resources in order to survive"* (Armstrong et al., 2021).

Collaboration between schools is facilitated by leaders who coordinate together, share responsibility and build capacity. Trust and clear communication foster the relationships that enable people to work together. A pre-existing culture of collaboration is also helpful. Partnerships that flourish have a strong focus on teaching and learning, shared values, dispersed leadership responsibility and a commitment to professional development.

What is Equity in education?

Equity in education is about supporting children who need it most. Students who become well-educated citizens are the foundation for stronger economies and more resilient societies.

Equity refers to the principle of fairness. *"Inequities occur when biased or unfair policies, programmes, practices, or situations contribute to a lack of equality in educational performance, results, and outcomes"* (The Glossary of Education Reform, 2016). Providing Equity in education requires honesty about inequality and its impact on individuals and society in the future. It entails a commitment to those with unique needs and those disadvantaged by systemic inequalities. What we have seen in recent years, and especially since the pandemic, is increasing inequality, and a growing gap in opportunities, attainments and life chances. Although this is happening globally, there are pockets of good practice everywhere.

What is happening internationally

Creating equitable provision for diverse student populations is a key feature of education policy in OECD countries. Some countries appear to be doing much better for their children than others. Here are just two of many examples.

Finland

Since the 1980s, Finnish educators have focused on making education an instrument to balance out social inequality. Schools are not in competition with each other for who is 'best' or 'top,' as collaboration is the norm. The aim is to support each other to do well. Students often have the same teacher for up to six years of their education. During those years, mutual trust and bonding are built so that both parties know and respect each other. Pupil progress is tracked individually, with no standardized testing. There are no government inspections that grade schools against specific criteria.

Finland has consistently better educational outcomes for children than most across the world. This begins with generous entitlements and leave for new parents. Early years staff and teachers are graduates, well paid and highly respected. Only the best qualified become educators, and there is stiff competition. The curriculum is focused on learning through play, and formal education does not begin until children are 7 years old.

Estonia

Children do not start school in Estonia until 7 either, and every child is legally entitled to a kindergarten place from 18 months. Lunches, transport and textbooks are all free. Classes are mixed ability, and pupils are not routinely separated into sets. Exclusions are virtually unheard of, and most young people stay in education until they are 19. Schools are the best at promoting fairness, and Estonian pupils are amongst the happiest in the world. The government trusts teachers, and both educators and schools have a high degree of autonomy. There is an emphasis on problem-solving, critical thinking, values, entrepreneurship and digital competence, skills employers want. According to the OECD Programme for International Student Assessment, Estonia has the best education system in Europe.

Equity in practice in the early years

Children learn more in the first five years of their life than at any other time. The synaptic connections in their brains are growing by up to a million a second. What happens at home, in playgroup, kindergarten or other early years setting is critical for their understanding not only of the world around them but also their sense of self. For those who come from disadvantaged or challenging circumstances, this is the time when the most difference can be made to their future. The skills and approaches of early years practitioners are vital in this endeavour, and these need to be valued much more highly than they currently are.

These early years of life make all the difference to life trajectories. What happens in early years settings is vital to Equity. The older children become, the more intractable the inequities – and the harder it becomes to close the gap. So how can we best make the most of the opportunities the early years presents.

Family support

A valuable aspect of the Sure Start centres was the support given to parents. This made a positive difference to their relationship with their child and enhanced the home learning environment. This good practice will be replicated in many ways in early years settings.

Reach Children's Hub

An initiative in the Feltham area of West London is aimed at supporting new families and their babies. The focus is on reducing parental stress, promoting positive mental and physical health and wellbeing, encouraging social connections and sharing evidence-based information:

- Meeting families in pregnancy and providing free classes that focus on health and wellbeing
- Providing free antenatal education classes to develop parents' ability to make informed decisions
- Connecting postnatal parents through WhatsApp groups and drop-in weekly coffee mornings
- Providing five-week baby massage courses to support parents in using nurturing touch with their babies
- Offering tailored, one-to-one and group support to encourage and develop early language and promote positive, nurturing play techniques
- Leading postnatal 'walk and talks'.

Talking, reading and thinking

Literacy is one of the best predictors of later educational attainment, and gaps are already apparent at 12 months. Before literacy comes language. There are now many anecdotes, especially since the pandemic, of children who arrive in school with severely impoverished language. Parents do not always realise that talking with their babies and young children helps grow their brains. Infants may also spend a lot of time in front of screens that do not offer human interaction. Campaigns to help parents understand the importance of talking, singing and interacting with their children from the very earliest days of life would not only be immensely beneficial to the children but would also reinforce parents' view of themselves as their child's first and most important teachers.

Tuning into the sounds babies make, not just their cries for attention, could help in understanding how language develops and the steps towards cognitive development and learning. There are separate areas in the brain for receptive language (understanding) and expressive language (speaking). Receptive comes first. Unless children have many opportunities to hear language in context, their speaking will be delayed. It doesn't matter which language – it is better for children to become fluent in their home language first, as this gives them the tools to think; second language learning is then easier. Children can, however, cope well with becoming bilingual when they hear both languages on a regular basis. These are just a few ways that encourage stronger parent-child conversation.

- Tell babies what is happening: "I am just going to change your nappy now, let's lift up your legs – well done". Sing to them, tell them they are precious and loved!
- Rather than take the opportunity to chat with friends on the phone, talk with children in the playground: "Would you like to go higher on the swing?" "What shall we make in the sandpit?"
- Regularly point out words for things when children have visual cues: "There's a boy on a bike". "We need some tomatoes, shall we have big ones like these or little ones over there?"

- Ask toddlers for help: "Can you fetch that cloth for me?" "Thank you for being helpful"
- Count whenever the opportunity arises – going up stairs, buttons on coats, pieces of toast on a plate.
- Talk together about the cartoons children watch rather than just put them in front of a screen – even just asking what the story was about or their favourite character.
- Ask children to make small choices – do you want to wear these red trousers or those green ones?
- Give children information about changes: "I am going to work now, bye-bye, see you later".
- Thank children for tidying up, helping, sharing, eating their dinner – be specific so children know exactly why you are pleased.
- Asking children what they enjoyed the most at the end of the day is a way of promoting a positive mindset.

Not all parents will have good literacy skills themselves, so suggesting they read stories to their children might be a non-starter. Having family story/singing sessions a couple of times a week could help parents understand what children gain from these experiences and why they matter for their healthy development and future learning.

Some early years – and primary – settings have introduced a family room where parents can meet, have a hot drink together and receive information (in community translations where needed) about local services.

Toy libraries

Families struggling with bills for food and heating may not be able to buy toys for their children, and this may make them feel inadequate as parents. The benefits of toy libraries based in early years settings not only come from providing a selection of toys but also information on how they might promote various aspects of development. Of course, young children might get attached to certain toys and want to keep them. It is probably worth saying that toys can be returned when children no longer play with them rather than demanding them back! Many people would be happy to donate toys their children have grown out of if they knew of the need and how to do this.

Behaviour

It is when a child begins to establish their identity and independence that the warm glow of having a baby is replaced by an entirely different set of feelings! Two- and 3-year-olds can be both challenging and exhausting. Many parents do not know how to cope with non-compliance and toddlers' fierce expressions of distress at the slightest provocation, and may resort to practices that are harmful, both to the children themselves and to relationships. This is a tricky time for families. Early years centres can provide both practical guidance and emotional support.

Parents/carers need the following:

- Information about what different behaviours mean for healthy, natural development
- To know that they are not alone in struggling with the demands of this age group
- Acknowledgement that difficult behaviour is exacerbated by tiredness, hunger, insufficient warning of activity change, and having too much sugar
- Awareness that children may react strongly to uncertainty or changes at home, such as family conflict and/or separation, the absence of someone close and even new siblings. Talking with children at a level they can understand will help

- To reassure children they are loved, even though you are telling them their behaviour is unacceptable, maintains positive relationships
- To use I statements with the positive, as they are easier for children to hear. For example: "I need you to put your shoes on now", rather than, "You can't go out without your shoes", and they might be more willing to comply – eventually!
- To show children what is needed: "I am going to put my shoes on now, first me, then you"
- To keep things light-hearted where possible: "Goodness, I think I have my shoes on the wrong feet – don't they look funny? You tell me if I have got your shoes on properly"
- To give children elements of control and choice where possible: "Do you want to wear your boots or your trainers today?"
- To promote positive behaviour by being clear, calm, consistent, collaborative, caring and constructive: even though this is not always easy, it is less wearing than reacting to challenges all the time
- To give children attention and positive feedback for wanted behaviour; this is more effective than giving attention to unwanted behaviour – any attention is rewarding
- To understand the power of positive role models – children see, children hear, children copy
- To use the language of strengths to help the child develop a positive self-concept
- To learn about emotional regulation and what to do to help children cope with difficult feelings – especially acknowledging why they are upset and giving them the language to express how they feel
- To find emotional support for themselves – it is really hard for parents to cope well with a demanding and difficult toddler when they are depleted. Just telling them they are doing a good job in difficult circumstances may help
- To accept practical support when needed – sometimes this can be just putting parents in touch with each other.

Attention skills

Children are often overwhelmed with things to pay attention to and may find it hard to learn to focus. Turning the television off and restricting the use of a phone or tablet reduces the level of stimuli in the environment. When children have many toys to choose from, they can be indecisive because they are spoiled for choice. It is easier for them to have a small selection rather than all of them.

Gender

It is in the early years that gender identification and discrimination begin. You only have to walk around a toy shop or even a card shop to realise how powerful this is. Pink and blue are just for starters!

Entrenched stereotyped gender roles can limit opportunities for both males and females. When activities are gender neutral in the early years setting, both boys and girls can make choices based on interest – not on what they believe they 'should' be playing with. There are two specific ways of reducing bias.

1 Avoiding the default position of labelling animals, toys and other items as male. So often children hear 'he, him and his' when the alternative of 'she, her and hers' is just as valid.
2 Regularly extending the images that children inevitably bring with them, such as princesses and superheroes. Asking what superpowers the princesses have and mentioning that Spiderman needs to wash his spider suit for the next adventure are just two examples of what is possible.

The conversations that staff have with children make a difference to their freedom of 'becoming'. Ultimately this also changes how they think about themselves in the world. Encouragement to express emotions safely is valuable, not just as an early step in emotional regulation but in future when it supports mental health.

Equity in practice in the primary classroom

Equity is when each individual has what they need and has the same opportunities for success as others. This means both taking barriers away and putting things in place. In the classroom, some students might be given extra time, different supports or specific resources to maximise their learning outcomes.

Although Equity is largely the responsibility of schools, school systems and educational policies, there are things primary classroom teachers can do to promote flexibility and fairness.

Oracy

> *It is our ability to communicate that enables us to build positive relationships, collaborate for common purpose, deliberate and share our ideas as citizens. It is through speaking and listening that we develop our views, apply knowledge and extend our capacity to think critically.*
>
> (Millard & Menzies, n.d.)

Talking is a fundamental skill, but it often takes second place to literacy in schools. It has outcomes beyond the classroom that can benefit students far into their future, including positive relationships and work opportunities. A focus on oracy helps students discuss topics with others, explore their understanding, develop confidence in their ideas and present their findings. As we have already heard, many young children often do not get the opportunity to develop good language skills, so this needs to be a central plank of primary education for all pupils. Even when children are doing well academically, they may lack confidence in sharing their ideas, so this benefits everyone, not just those who are disadvantaged.

Teaching and learning oracy

Oracy is not a specific lesson but is threaded through everyday interactions. It is as much about modelling and structured opportunities as direct input. Both the depth and breadth of vocabulary matter. Children need to know what words mean and the contexts in which to use them and have access to alternatives that allow them to be more specific in their descriptions and communicate subtlety. Language in the classroom needs to become increasingly sophisticated, with new words explained and then used frequently until they become embedded in children's vocabulary. Children who are the 'weather monitors' become the 'meteorologists'; 'friendly' becomes 'empathic, 'considerate' or 'supportive'; and writing becomes 'documenting', recording or summarising. Oracy is aligned with cooperative learning in that pupils need to talk to each other to develop and communicate their ideas. When teachers ask for contributions from a whole class, it is the already confident and able children who are most likely to answer, which does not raise the ability nor confidence of others.

> *Oracy is a powerful tool for learning; by teaching students to become more effective speakers and listeners we empower them to better understand themselves, each other and the world around them. It is also a route to social mobility, empowering all students, not just some, to find their voice to succeed in school and life.*
>
> (Voice 21)

Demonstrating knowledge

Traditionally, students were asked to write individual essays, but that is very limiting with today's breadth of possibilities. Alternatives may be individual, paired and cooperative group efforts which could include podcasts, videos, PowerPoint presentations, mind maps, posters or presentations incorporating drama.

Cooperative learning

This is based on a set of principles and techniques that enable students to effectively collaborate with each other. These include the following:

- Random groupings, so that students collaborate with a wide range of peers – this enriches learning, facilitates new perspectives and seeks strengths in others
- Teaching basic collaborative skills, such as asking for help, offering suggestions, giving feedback, responding positively to others' ideas and efforts, managing different viewpoints without conflict, following up on suggestions and showing pride in achievements
- Reliance on group members first before asking the teacher
- Equal opportunities to participate – each person has a role, and no one is excluded
- All students are expected to contribute and are accountable to the rest of the group for what they offer to the joint project: no one can opt-out
- Interdependence means that what benefits one person will benefit the group, and what is damaging to one pupil affects the group
- Cooperation is seen as a value that improves the lives of individuals, groups, whole communities and society.

Collaborative activities could include research, project development, presentation to the class.

When students use collaborative skills, their groups are likely to function better (Soller, 2001), leading to more learning and more enjoyment of learning.

Teaching and learning adaptations

Many children have a struggle in school and will need a flexible response to be able to make the most of being there. The first thing is to ask students what is most helpful to them in their learning. Most will be able to come up with their own ideas. Some pupils need more time to complete a piece of work, or the parameters of the task may be changed so that they achieve a section of it. This makes for depth rather than breadth but makes it more likely students will learn something rather than skim it. Scaffolding a task into smaller manageable steps also ensures that the pupil sees themselves making progress in their learning rather than attempting and failing at something out of reach. Some students also need more opportunities than others to practice something new until it becomes secure and they can apply or generalise it. It may be useful to give some students prior information before introducing a new topic so they already have some knowledge when it is introduced to the rest of the class. This may include new words as well as new concepts.

Sometimes it is helpful to involve parents in this but not always. It depends on the demands on families and how they interpret any request for support. Some may know how to make new learning fun, while others may put pressure on children that increases their anxiety.

Environmental adaptations

Some students will need a quieter, less distracting place to sit in the classroom; others may need to be at the front. Pupils who do not feel secure in English may benefit from being with others who speak their language and can help translate.

When all students feel accepted and welcomed into the class, whatever their backgrounds and needs, they will be more willing to engage. It is worth checking in with all pupils from time to time to see whether initial adaptations are still useful or need changing.

Glasses in Classes

Studies have shown that there is a link between poor eyesight and reduced literacy scores. It is recommended that all children in England receive an eyesight test in their reception year. Roughly 10%–15% of children fail this eyesight test, and of these, around a third are not taken to the opticians to obtain glasses. The Glasses in Classes intervention aims to address this by linking schools, families, opticians and health services, especially in areas of disadvantage known as 'Opportunity Areas'. Children who need glasses are given two free pairs, one to take home and one to keep in school.

At the start of the Opportunity Area programme in 2017, pupils in Bradford were 6.2 percentage points behind the national average in reading at Key Stage 2. That gap narrowed almost a third to 4.6 percentage points in 2018 and halved to 3.1 percentage points in 2019.

The 'Glasses in Classes' scheme is being adapted for five disadvantaged areas in England. This will reach more than 9,000 pupils in at least 225 schools.

Citizenship in action

Children need to experience having a say in what concerns them, not just have things imposed on them. This aligns with Agency and also underpins the understanding that everyone has both a voice and a responsibility for ensuring things are fair. This is the basis of a functioning democracy. Here are three ideas for putting citizenship in action.

1 *Sharing responsibility:* At the beginning of the school year, children work in small groups (possibly in a Circle session) to make a list of what jobs need doing in the class. Teacher input may be needed, but they promote thinking rather than telling. Once they have decided, different groups are given one of those tasks and asked to write a job description – what needs to be done, how often and to what standard. Pupils work in pairs to fulfil the jobs, partly because that is more fun and they can talk to each other, also so that if one is absent, the other can make sure it happens. They can ask for help if needed. Jobs change every half-term to give everyone opportunities to take responsibility for different tasks. In the first instance, pupils volunteer. Those who do not get this responsibility the first time around will get a turn later. For the more unpopular jobs, names may need to be pulled from a hat! Not all students will have a job every half-term. Who does what is written up on the classroom wall.
2 *Classroom Culture:* This is an alternative to imposed class rules. The idea was given to me by a primary school teacher in Australia who said that behaviour in his class was much improved when students had a voice and choice. At the beginning of the school year, the teacher puts up at least 25 values onto the wall of the class with enough room for children to put a tick. These can include kindness, punctuality, courtesy, listening, patience,

helpfulness, honesty and support. The students have ten votes and a week to vote for what they want in their class that year. They can use all votes on one value if they want. At the end of this exercise, the teacher takes the most values with the most votes and turns these into a code of conduct for the class – framed on the positive.

3 *Democracy:* If the school has a student representative council or the equivalent, then each class needs to be represented, preferably by two students. Individuals stand as candidates and say what is important to them and how they will represent the views of the class. Everyone has a confidential vote. The elected representatives meet every half-term with the whole class to report on actions, seek information on what is important to pupils in order to raise it and give fellow pupils opportunities to ask questions. The class could also elect two observers whose job it is to attend Student Council meetings but without being able to vote.

Equity in practice across the primary school

Children from disadvantaged households are more likely to experience poor early learning. This results in greater risks to later academic attainment, employment and civic engagement. But some children with high early risk factors do well, demonstrating that equitable outcomes are possible – we can create a more level playing field for all children.

Physical care

It is hard for children to be active learners when they are hungry, tired, sick, cold or scared, so their physical wellbeing has to be a priority. Breakfast clubs are not a luxury in education when children have not been fed at home. Some families find it hard to make sure their children get enough sleep, so when a child puts their head down in school, the best thing to do is find them a place of rest. This not only enables the child to catch up on missed sleep but also shows care from adults. Conversations with all parents about the importance of good quality sleep and a discussion about how best to do this might be valuable at the beginning of every year – or even every term.

Relationships with families

Often, the bonds that early years practitioners form with families weaken as children go through school. But there are good reasons for maintaining positive two-way communications:

- Parents may be reluctant to talk about what is happening at home, but when children's learning and behaviour deteriorates, teachers need to understand why, so they do not jump to judgment and can support children through difficult times. This can be clarified when children are first registered at a school, so that requests do not appear out of the blue. Reassure families that information will be kept confidential, but it is in the child's best interests for teachers to know about anything that may be affecting their concentration, learning and/or behaviour.
- Families can learn about services and benefits they might need.
- Inviting parents to watch short videos about their children's learning and positive ways to support that at home can also be valuable and does not depend on having fluent literacy skills. This can also give families opportunities to talk with each other as well as with staff.

Strength through Diversity

The OECD's Strength through Diversity Project identifies the following six steps that incorporate what needs to happen at both a policy and practice level in schools to maximise Equity and Inclusion. The following is a summary:

- Policymakers need to question how education systems are governed, resourced and monitored to ensure they reflect the needs of *all* students.
- Funding models need to be designed with the explicit goal of fostering Equity and Inclusion. Regular and targeted funding should be balanced to avoid the multiplication of programmes, a lack of coordination and inefficiencies.
- Teachers and school leaders need Equity and Inclusion as core themes in initial and continuous professional learning. This fosters an understanding of how to address diversity in the classroom.
- All relevant stakeholders – students, parents, teacher unions, specific organisations – should be engaged to help promote equitable and inclusive policies. This will raise awareness of diversity issues, as well as create more positive classroom environments.
- Schools should identify and address the needs of students in each classroom. An Individual Education Plan can be developed and progress monitored. Schools can also support students through access to psychological services.
- Education systems need to be flexible and responsive to the needs of students. This can happen by providing different paths, such as providing academic and vocational choices, offering an inclusive curriculum, and adopting a range of teaching formats from one-on-one tuition to small-group approaches.

Students with special educational needs and disabilities (SEND)

SEND education is about Equity, not equality, because education must be fair to every individual but it cannot always be the same.

Paul Harris (2019)

Where education systems are based on age rather than developmental needs, and teachers are expected to deliver a one-size-fits-all curriculum, Inclusion in mainstream schools is inevitably more of a challenge for both pupils and educators. A rights-based approach to learning, however, says that children with additional needs have the right to be educated alongside their peers, including the right to make progress. This means creating the conditions that facilitate individual learning in an inclusive rather than segregated setting. Putting this into practice entails commitment to the children, careful planning, close liaison with both families and professionals, professional learning for teachers, and flexibility. Although beliefs and perspectives are free, support can be expensive. Resource allocation is not always up to individual schools but dictated by the systems in which they are operating, so Equity can be elusive. It is not surprising that families often believe that they have to 'fight' for their children where funds are limited. Those who are more knowledgeable about how systems work, and have the resources to pay for professional support, are at an advantage in a competitive environment, entrenching further inequalities.

There have been university faculties devoted to Inclusion for children with disabilities, and the issue is both complex and not without controversy. There are those, for instance, who reject the term 'special' needs, saying that everyone has needs that require meeting in different ways. The social model of disability differs from the medical model in saying that people are disabled by their environment and that once provision is in place they can have many of the opportunities offered to others. This is powerfully illustrated by issues of access.

Access

If you have ever needed to use a wheelchair, you will know that there are places you cannot go, things you cannot do and experiences you cannot have because there is no provision for someone in a wheelchair. The need for adaptation to the environment applies to anyone who is otherwise unable to participate in what is on offer for everyone else. In a school, this means enabling access to a full learning experience for everyone. Some enablers will entail cost, but many will be simply doing things differently.

In Australia, the Human Rights Commission lists 31 ways in which disabled students might be denied full access to education and what might help (see resources at the end of the chapter). The attitudes and beliefs of educators, as well as policymakers, are critical.

According to the Disabled Living Foundation, there are 800,000 pupils in the UK with a disability, and the majority attend mainstream schools. Under the *Equality Act 2010*, all schools in the UK are required to have an accessibility plan. Following an access audit, this plan should include how the school aims to:

- Increase the extent to which pupils with disabilities can participate in the curriculum
- Improve the physical environment to enable pupils with disabilities to take better advantage of the education, benefits, facilities and services provided
- Improve the availability of accessible information – not just in writing but using one or more other formats.

This is not just about buildings and books but asking pupils (and their families) what they need and what works for them. 'One-size-fits-all' is not applicable to special needs any more than it is to other young people.

Inclusive design

Inclusive design, usually considered in relation to the built environment, places people at the heart of the process, acknowledges human diversity and offers dignity, autonomy and choice.

The principles are based on the social model where the 'problem' is not disabled people themselves but that individuals are made disabled by their environment, people's attitudes, policies and procedures.

Physical and some other disabilities are visible. Sometimes this can lead to exclusion or bullying but can also result in well-intentioned actions when the person is seen in the light of their disability and what they can't do, rather than a focus on the whole person and enabling adaptations that build independence. There are also hidden disabilities which may be harder to spot but also need flexible arrangements.

It is not just a small minority that need adaptations to access the learning environment. Acoustics for instance are not only an issue for those with limited hearing but also those with poor sight who rely on sound. Neurodiverse students may find noisy environments overwhelming.

These are just a few of the material adaptations needed in schools: There are many more:

- Step free or level access, with consideration also given to rugs, play surfaces etc
- Assistive listening systems
- Interactive white boards with colours such as pink on dark blue which are more comfortable to read than black on white.

Children just want to be children, to fit in, to join in if they want to and as far as possible to be treated the same as everyone else. There is much that can be done to make this happen, but it takes an enabling perspective and a belief that it is worthwhile – not only for that individual in the here and now but also for the possibilities for their future.

Teresa Rumble, Senior Access Advisor and Inclusive Design Specialist, Centre for Accessible Environments, UK

As well as material adaptations, the knowledge and practices of educators are critical.

Conductive hearing loss

Due to the immaturity of the Eustachian tube, many children under the age of 7 have blocked ears when they have a cold, so although they can hear sounds, they cannot always make out the meaning of what is being said. This comes and goes and is often undiagnosed. Sometimes this leads to adults saying things like, "She hears me when she wants to!", rather than appreciating that the context gives clues. This has implications not just for communication but also attention, reading, behaviour and play. Children need contextual and visual support, including being able to lip-read instructions. Teachers of young children who are aware of this know that the way they position themselves when speaking can make a significant difference to a pupil's ability to access information. To facilitate lip-reading, a speaker needs to be in light, not shadow, and facing the listener.

How a child gets to school, the way classrooms are organised, groups are arranged and the expectations on both the child with disability and their peers are all relevant in making learning accessible.

To limit stereotyping, all pupils need awareness of people with a range of disabilities in a wide variety of roles. These include politicians, comedians, actors, scientists, academics, entrepreneurs and educators. The increased focus on the Paralympics in the last 20 years or so, as well as actors with disability being more visible, has given everyone a less restricted perspective. However 'normality' is defined, it should not be the only criteria for Inclusion and success.

Outside spaces

Both greener views and surroundings, as well as time spent within green spaces, offer children numerous mental, physical and social developmental benefits and spur their growth into ecologically aware and responsible citizens. Moreover, when equally accessible, green spaces serve to reduce the health inequities suffered by socio-economically disadvantaged children.

(UNICEF, 2021)

There is now a wealth of research (Burke et al., 2023; UNICEF, 2021) that confirms that wellbeing is enhanced by being in nature – in the open air in green and blue spaces. In some communities, there is little by way of open space at all, so it makes sense for schools, wherever possible, to arrange for pupils to visit parks, woods, countryside and seaside places, and if that is not possible, to find areas within the grounds where children can experience the natural world. Amongst other things, UNICEF suggests that schools:

- preserve, improve, create and maintain safe and accessible green spaces
- integrate environmental education into the curriculum so that children begin to understand how important it is to take care of the natural world
- set aside time for children to be outdoors during the day.

Behaviour

Loss

Children under 7 are at an ego-centric stage of their development and may believe that it is somehow their fault when someone in their lives disappears. Parents may be reluctant to talk to their young children about family breakdown, but it is critical that they do – without demonising the other parent, which may eventually backfire. Children need reassurance that they are not to blame and are not 'bad', and also that they are still loved. Children of any age may be confused, angry and coping with a high level of stress at home or emotional neglect as adults struggle themselves with the situation.

When someone is very ill and perhaps dies, children also need information at a level they can understand without using euphemisms such as 'going to sleep', which may leave imaginative minds frightened of going to bed.

In school, a sudden deterioration in pupil behaviour or reduced focus on learning is an indication that something is happening that is distressing them. A sensitive conversation with a parent asking for their insights may help. Letting the child know you are aware that things are tough for them at the moment but that some behaviours are still not acceptable is one way of handling difficulties. It is also a good idea to have as much of normal routine as possible so that something in the child's life is stable and reliable. Teachers do more than they know to provide a predictable and safe environment.

A valuable intervention is 'Seasons for Growth' (see resources): this is an early intervention peer support program based on the belief that change, loss and grief are a normal and valuable part of life. It is for any pupil who is dealing with major changes in their life. The program consists of 8 weekly sessions of 50 minutes duration, led by a trained group facilitator (a 'companion'), followed by a celebration session and two re-connector sessions. Using a Seasons metaphor to discuss change and growth, the group engages in games, discussion and creative activities. This helps children connect with others and reduce feelings of isolation, understand the process of grief and develop coping strategies.

Trauma

Many children live in stressful situations, but this is different from trauma, which is an experience outside normality that is overwhelming. It can result in hypervigilance, inability to sleep, flashbacks, terror, deep depression, helplessness and the need to re-assert control. Trauma experiences include family and community violence, serious accidents, physical and sexual abuse, refugee experiences, involvement in natural disasters and witnessing scenes of inhumanity. Some children who have experienced trauma may exhibit behaviour that is hard to manage. Some have a low tolerance for frustration and exhibit aggression, while others withdraw and/or regress. Sanctions for unwanted behaviour are meaningless for these students. Highly charged emotional distress leading to uncontrolled behaviours can be triggered by sights, sounds, smells, anniversaries or anything else that brings back memories of the trauma. Trauma-informed responses include the following:

- Refocusing the child into the here and now
- Reassuring them they are safe
- Identifying and removing potential triggers where possible
- Comforting the child and reminding them that they are not alone.

A trusting relationship between adult and child is the basis of effective intervention, but all educators need training and support when they have traumatised children in their care (see the chapter on Respect).

Equity in the staffroom

There is a wealth of information about Equity in the classroom, but little that addresses the same or similar issues in the staffroom. Gender inequality can be writ large in primary schools, where the majority of classroom teachers are female and senior leadership often male. Women take leave to have families, and although this can be seen as 'their choice', the support available to them and the expectation that men will not also take on parenting responsibilities are systemic and cultural. There is more gender Equity than there was, but women are still vulnerable to institutional discrepancies. There are also some institutions where not being white middle class, not speaking 'good' English or not having the same religion as others is a barrier to promotion. This may not be overt discrimination that is evident in policy and practice but a subtle and more covert aspect of a historically embedded culture. People in these schools may be reluctant to challenge prejudice for fear this might generate conflict.

Performance-related pay is a danger to Equity. It is usually a reward for pupils achieving high scores on tests. This puts value on only one aspect of a teacher's role and has the potential to create a toxic culture.

Equity in social and emotional learning (SEL)

Equity in Circle Solutions is achieved by everyone having the opportunity for a turn, even if they choose to 'pass'. No one is singled out. Over time, louder children become quieter and quieter children gain confidence. The teacher also joins in with all the activities that the children do. This provides a good model of expectations, promotes positive pupil-teacher relationships and shows that adults are also learning.

Activities in SEL

Strengths in Circles Cards:

There are seven statements for each of the six ASPIRE principles.
  These are three of those for Equity:

* We share what we have
* We stand up for what is fair
* We can all participate

In groups of three or four, all students are given one of these statements and discuss the following questions together.

– What does this mean?
– Is this what we want in our class?
– What would it make people feel about being here?
– Is it already happening – how do we know?
– What else might we do?

Each group decides on one action. They give a brief report back to the Circle, emphasising the action. What they all agree is put on display as a reminder.

Confidence Cake:

This is suitable for an upper primary class.

Confidence is what people need to have a go, to speak out and to not give up when they make a mistake.

In groups of three or four, children are given a large piece of paper and coloured pens. They are asked to think of ingredients that would be needed for a 'confidence cake'. How would they mix these ingredients, and what would be needed to make sure it was 'cooked'. Then how might they decorate it? After discussion, they draw the finished cake and write the recipe using amounts, such as "start with a kilo of … add a big handful of … a spoonful of … and a sprinkling of …", etc. The finished 'cakes' are put on display.

Step by Step to Speech

This intervention was initiated to support a 7-year-old child, Amina*, who was diagnosed with selective mutism – she didn't speak in class or the playground and would only communicate in occasional whispers with her teacher. Her reluctance appeared to emanate from a strict father who expected her to speak English, despite this not being her first language, and came down heavily on any mistake. Amina had very little confidence.

About eight children from different classes met weekly for a term with a support teacher.

Children were seated in a Circle including the teacher.

All children in the group completed the activity successfully three times before the next activity was attempted. No pressure was ever exerted – children joined in when they felt comfortable.

Activity One: Passing a smile around the Circle. They could also pass a frown, a surprised face, an angry face and a funny face! No sound was required – but it did make children laugh! The smile went one way and then the other.

Activity Two: Animal noises. There are many ways to do this. One is for the teacher to read a story about animals and ask all the children to make the animal noise when they appear in the book. Then each child is given an animal and makes the sound when their animal appears in the story. Songs like "Old MacDonald Had a Farm" also give children the opportunity to make animal noises.

Activity Three: Names: Children played Mexican wave – standing up in turn around the Circle and throwing their arms in the air. First silently, then saying their own name as they stood up.

When children knew each other's names, they could throw a ball to someone in the Circle and call their name as they did this. There are many variations on this theme.

Activity Four: Single words. Using a 'talking stick' children went around the Circle with a single-word answer to a simple sentence stem that the teacher introduces. Although pupils usually gave answers based on their own lives and preferences, they were not asked to. Giving children a minute to think of their answer was helpful. The teacher modelled what to do by going first. These are examples of sentence stems.

- The nicest food to eat is ...
- Babies are ...
- Football is ...
- Going shopping can be ...
- Happiness is ...

Activity Five: Pair shares and sentences: Children were mixed up in a game and then worked with a partner. They were given a simple task, such as thinking about what they both liked to do at the weekend or a cartoon they both watched, something they had in common. They then reported back to the Circle, beginning their sentence, "We ..."

At the end of this activity, which was carried out over a term, Amina was playing and interacting with children in the playground and, although still shy, was able to verbally answer questions in class.

(* Name has been changed)

Equity checklist

	This is in place – we know it is effective because ...	Working on it – our actions to date are ...	Just started – our next step will be ...
All staff believe that every child can learn and has potential			
All staff believe that every child has a right to education			
Policies and practices acknowledge the need for flexibility			
Policies and practices respect the need for fairness			
Collaboration is encouraged			
Staff have access to professional development on meeting the needs of diverse learners			
The school and learning are accessible to all			
	This is in place – we know it is effective because ...	Working on it – our actions to date are ...	Just started – our next step will be ...

Equity in the future

'Levelling up' has become a catchphrase that looks good in political manifestos but means nothing unless there is action to make this happen. We cannot talk about tax cuts and social equality in the same breath. Ensuring that all children have opportunities to flourish means funding state education so that all schools have the infrastructure they need to meet diverse needs.

Professor Richard Wilkinson, co-author of *The Spirit Level* (2010), asserts that greater social equality is the most important factor in ensuring people's wellbeing. In contrast to less equal rich countries, more equal rich countries have, for example:

- Higher levels of education
- More trust and community involvement
- Greater social mobility
- More wellbeing among children
- Lower levels of physical ill health
- Lower levels of mental ill health
- Less drug abuse
- Lower rates of imprisonment
- Less obesity
- Less violence
- Fewer teenage births.

Societies with a bigger gap between the rich and the poor are bad for everyone in them, including the well-off. While greater equality yields the greatest benefits for the poor, the benefits extend to the majority of the population.

What we have learnt throughout this chapter is that a one-size-fits-all education does not meet the needs of many children. Some have chronic disadvantages, while others have issues in their lives which impact on their learning or behaviour at a given time. Giving learners greater capacity and flexibility to determine their educational pathways according to their evolving contexts, interests and needs gives them the best chance of reaching their potential – maximising opportunity and therefore enhancing Equity. This may require education systems to become more dynamic in the face of economic and societal challenges.

For a nation to thrive and for the future to be secure so that everyone has the best chance to live life well, we need to change direction from focusing on what is good just for *me* to what is better for *us*.

References, further reading and resources

Armstrong, P.W., Brown, C. & Chapman, C.J. (2021). School-to-school collaboration in England: A configurative review of the empirical evidence. *Review of Education*, 9, 319–351.

Burke, J., Clarke, D., O'Keeffe, J. & Meehan, T. (2023). The impact of blue and green spaces on wellbeing: A review of reviews through a positive psychology lens. *Journal of Happiness and Health*, 3(2), 93–108.

Cattan. S., Contil, G., Farquaharson, C., Ginja, R and Pecher, M. (2021). *The Health Impacts of Sure Start*. The Institute of Fiscal Studies. https://www.ifs.org.uk/publications/health-impacts-sure-start

Gaheer, S. & Paull, G. (2016). *The Value for Money of Children's Centre Services: Evaluation of Children's Centres in England (ECCE) Strand 5*. Department for Education, Research Report.

Galtung, J. (1969). Violence, peace, and peace research. *Journal of Peace Research*, 6(3), 167–191.

Galtung, J. (1990). Cultural violence. *Journal of Peace Research*, 27(3), 291–305.

The Glossary of Education Reform (2016). https://www.edglossary.org

Harris, P. (2019). SEND education should be about Equity, not equality. *Education Executive.*

Heckman, J. (n.d.) *Invest in Early Childhood Development: Reduce Deficits, Strengthen the Economy.* https://www.heckmanequation.org/resource/invest-in-early-childhood-development-reduce-deficits-strengthen-the-economy/

Lerner, M.J. (1980). *The Belief in a Just World: A Fundamental Delusion.* Springer.

Millard, W. & Menzies, L. (n.d.) The State of Speaking in our Schools: https://www.voice21.org/wp-content/uploads/2019/10/Voice-21-State-of-speaking-in-our-schools.pdf

Royal Foundation Centre for Early Childhood. (2021). *Big Change Starts Small.* RFCfEC. https://www.centreforearlychildhood.org/report/

Sacker, M.E., Lacey, R. & Maughn, B. (2021). *The Lifelong Health and Wellbeing Trajectories of People who have been in Care.* Nuffield Foundation.

Seldon, A. & Sylvester, R. (Chairs) (2022). *Times Education Commission: Bringing Out the Best. How to transform education and unleash the potential of every child.* https://www.documentcloud.org/documents/22056664-times-education-commission-final-report

Soller, A. (2001). Supporting social interaction in an intelligent collaborative learning system. *International Journal of Artificial Intelligence in Education, 12,* 40–62.

UNICEF Armenia (2021). https://www.unicef.org/armenia/en/stories/necessity-urban-green-space-childrens-optimal-development

Voice21. (n.d.). https://www.voice21.org

Wilkinson, R. & Pickett, K. (2010). *The Spirit Level: Why equality is better for everyone.* Penguin Books.

Other sources and further reading

Aynsley-Green, A. (2019). *The British Betrayal of Childhood: Challenging uncomfortable truths and bringing out change.* Routledge.

Bronfenbrenner, U. (1979). *The ecology of human development: Experiences by nature and design.* Cambridge, MA: Harvard University Press.

Brunzell, T. & Norrish, J. (2021). *Creating Trauma-Informed, Strengths-Based Classrooms. Teacher strategies for nurturing students healing, growth and learning.* Jessica Kingsley.

Herrick, C. & Bell, K. (2022). Concepts, disciplines and politics: on 'structural violence' and the 'social determinants of health'. *Critical Public Health, 32*(3), 295–308.

Krammer, S.M.S., Lashitew, A.A., Doh, J.P. & Bapuji, H. (2023). Income inequality, social cohesion, and crime against businesses: Evidence from a global sample of firms. *Journal of International Business Studies, 54,* 385–400.

Lane, H.B. & Allen, S. (2010). The Vocabulary-Rich Classroom: Modeling Sophisticated Word Use to Promote Word Consciousness and Vocabulary Growth. *The Reading Teacher, 63*(5), 362–370.

Leadsom, A. (2021). *The Best Start for Life: A Vision for the 1,001 Critical Days.* Early Years Healthy Development Review Report, Department of Health and Social Care.

Quinlan, D. & Roffey, S. (2021). Positive Education with Disadvantaged Students. In M.L. Kern & M.L. Wehmeyer (Eds) *The Palgrave Handbook of Positive Education.* Springer.

NSPCC (2023). https://www.learning.nspcc.org.uk/children-and-families-at-risk/looked-after-children

OECD (2020a). *Mapping policy approaches and practices for the inclusion of students with special education needs.* OECD Education Working Paper Number 227.

OECD (2020b). *The impact of Covid-19 on student Equity and inclusion: Supporting vulnerable students during school closures and reopenings.* https://www.oecd.org/coronavirus/policy-responses/the-impact-of-covid-19-on-student-equity-and-inclusion-supporting-vulnerable-students-during-school-closures-and-school-re-openings-d593b5c8/

OECD (2023). https://www.oecdedutoday.com/equity-and-inclusion-in-education/

Riley, A. (2012). Exploring the effects of the 'Seasons for Growth' intervention for pupils experiencing change and loss. *Educational and Child Psychology, 29*(3), 38–53.

Roffey, S. (2006). *Helping with Behaviour in the Early Years*. Routledge.

Roffey, S. (2019). *The Primary Behaviour Cookbook*. Routledge.

Roffey, S. & Parry, J. (2013). *Special Needs in the Early Years: Promoting Collaboration, Communication and Co-ordination*. 3rd edition. Routledge.

Rose, R. (Ed) (2010). *Confronting Obstacles to Inclusion: International Responses to Developing Inclusive Education*. Routledge.

Villanueva, K., Badland, H., Hooper, P., Javad, M.K., Mavoa, S., Davern, M., Roberts, R., Goldfeld, S. & Giles-Corti, B. (2015). Developing indicators of public open space to promote health and wellbeing in communities. *Applied Geography*, *57*, 112–119.

Weigart, K.M. (2008). Structural Violence. In L.R. Kurtz (Ed), *Encyclopaedia of Violence, Peace and Conflict*. Elsevier.

Resources

OECD:

- https://www.oecd.org/stories/education-equity/
- https://www.cascaid.co.uk/article/equity-in-education/

Voice 21 is the UK's oracy education charity. https://www.voice21.org

Equity for Children: https://www.equityforchildren.org/

Department for Children, Schools and Families. (2009). *Improving the Attainment of Looked After Children in Primary Schools* – excellent, historical practice in schools around the UK. https://www.assets.publishing.service.gov.uk/media/5a7b1d38e5274a319e77d1df/01047-2009.pdf

Seasons for Growth: an early intervention program to help children through grief, loss and major changes in their lives. https://www.seasonsforgrowth.co.uk/

Stories of disabled people and their fight for Equity and access: https://www.wearealldisabled.org/

Lifting Limits: this organisation works with schools to challenge gender stereotypes https://www.liftinglimits.org.uk/

Reading Rockets: this has great ideas about how to extend the vocabulary of young children using classroom tasks – from feeding the hamster to providing nutrition to our friendly rodent! https://www.readingrockets.org/topics/vocabulary/articles/vocabulary-rich-classroom-modeling-sophisticated-word-use-promote-word

7 ASPIRE in action across the world

This final chapter illustrates the application of the ASPIRE principles in educational settings across the world and the impact this has on learning, wellbeing and school culture. Although there are vibrant examples of each principle throughout the book, it is when they are all threaded through everything that happens across the school community that sustainable change happens. This not only impacts the learning and wellbeing of children, but also the wellbeing and efficacy of teachers. There are indications that ASPIRE also promotes positive engagement with the wider community. Step by step, we are beginning to create a brighter world.

School leaders and their vision for education

Positive education begins with a vision that encompasses the whole child in every aspect of their development and every child regardless of their ability, background or need. It is concerned with wellbeing as well as learning and how that learning takes place. Positive education also addresses school culture, how teachers feel about their profession, its challenges and rewards and whether families and diverse communities also feel they belong.

It is school leaders who have the most influence as change agents in a school. They need to be able to communicate their vision clearly and succinctly in ways which enable the whole community to believe in these values and this way of being. Having credibility and behaving in alignment with their vision helps school leaders to do this successfully. There will always be dissenting voices which need to be acknowledged and respected, but conversations change culture, and once this reaches a critical point and people can see for themselves the positive differences being experienced, then people will either get on board or leave.

Building a Positive school culture in Australia

I first met Jason Miezis when doing research in Australia on what was involved in creating an 'emotionally literate school'. He was the then principal of Rouse Hill Public School and his focus on the positive was in evidence everywhere. A laminated poster announcing "This is a No Put-Down Zone" was in every classroom, corridor, hall, the school office, principal's office and staff room. Pupils told me that they did not have bullying in their school because "we've got this no put-down thing". Teachers told me that Jason's positivity was infectious, and they clearly appreciated his approach because he walked the talk. While I was interviewing staff before school, he was busy with a barbecue, making them breakfast. Even staff who at first were cynical had come around to his way of thinking. Clearly it was having a positive impact on wellbeing for staff, as well as students; the sickness budget for the school was regularly underspent – giving more options for professional development activities.

DOI: 10.4324/9781003428237-8

This is an excerpt from a newsletter where Jason was also Principal:

We often refer to the term 'wellbeing' at our school. Wellbeing is a term used in all industries, but in an educational context, wellbeing centres on schools creating teaching and learning environments that enable students to be healthy, engaged and successful. The Department of Education has a Wellbeing Framework for Schools which provides teachers with a scaffold to ensure students' needs in the areas of cognitive, emotional, social, physical and spiritual wellbeing are maximised. We all want our students to be connected, successful and to thrive with their learning. At Cherrybrook Public School, the care, courtesy and love that teachers show for students is evident on a daily basis. I feel very proud to lead a team of delightful staff members who want students to thrive, flourish, do well and, as our school motto suggests, learn and grow.

With thanks to Jason Miezis, former Principal of Rouse Hill and Cherrybrook Public Schools, New South Wales.

Early years

Throughout the book we have emphasised the importance of what happens during a child's earliest interactions and the experiences they and their families have in an early years centre, whether this is a nursery, playgroup, preschool or kindergarten. Here, Rachel Berry explores how the ASPIRE principles are enacted in a project to engage young children with the natural environment.

Environmental Education and ASPIRE in the UK

Research has proven what we've always instinctively known: that nature is good for us. Walking in the forest lowers blood pressure and heart rate (Liu et al., 2021) and simply viewing images of natural landscapes induces states of relaxation (Jo et al., 2022). The same is true for children. Outdoor learning has been shown to improve wellbeing, resilience, academic achievement and behavioural self-regulation (McCree et al., 2020).

In my experience as a primary school teacher and early years educator, when children play in nature, they instinctively enact the principles of ASPIRE. Negotiating decisions in collaborative free play fosters respect and inclusivity. Connecting with each other and with living things develops compassion and curiosity. Exploration of the natural environment fosters agency and a sense of place. In terms of equity, nature is a great leveller, enabling individual strengths to come to the fore. Children flourish in the natural environment.

Wild Plots – a whole school, community-focused approach to ASPIRE through environmental education

One area we can address in schools is the reduction in numbers of pollinating insects which are vital for food production and plant reproduction. Wild Plots is one way to develop children's social and emotional learning through environmental awareness and taking action.

Stage 1: Having learnt about the importance of pollinators children will be tasked with identifying patches of land – could be a garden, a hanging basket or a scrubby patch next to the bus stop. Community involvement is key here, with lots of opportunities for writing letters, making posters and flyers, inviting speakers and visitors to the school to spread the word. Pollinators need help!

Stage 2: Children carry out surveys at their plot which could vary in sophistication, from counting how many pollinators they can count in a minute, to 1m quadrat surveys.

Stage 3: Children plan how to enhance the habitat by, for example, providing insect 'hotels', planting seeds or plug plants.

Stage 4: Carry out regular visits to observe changes, to develop a connection with their plot. They can also visit other areas that are being developed by other groups in the school.

Stage 5: Towards the end of the academic year, children re-survey their plot, collate their findings, then have a community celebration!

The project aims to build a positive school community and develop relationships beyond the school boundary, into the wider community. Everyone works together with a shared purpose. Through mutual effort and shared respect for the natural world, a hopeful future is created.

Rachel Berry

Social and emotional learning (SEL)

Social and emotional learning is where children think about who they want to become, the values that support their wellbeing and the relationships that enhance their lives and the health of their communities and the planet. SEL is included in every chapter because this gives children opportunities to engage with the ASPIRE principles in a way that encourages discussion, reflection and sometimes action. It is not just what we teach that matters, however, but how we do it. Circle Solutions is a framework for SEL that incorporates the ASPIRE principles as a pedagogy to ensure that this is a safe, solution-focused, strengths-based space for both teachers and learners. Circle Solutions is not a stand-alone intervention but, as Lily Liu illustrates here, a tool for wellbeing across the school.

Circle Solutions in China

The Covid epidemic profoundly impacted children's mental health worldwide. As the principal of Dehong Chinese International School in Xian, I needed something to support social and emotional learning for all our students. Since 2020 we have used the principles and methods of Circle Solutions and incorporated these into our curriculum. I want to share the positive impact this has had on our school's students, teachers and administrators.

Circle Solutions helps our students establish positive connections, enhances their confidence, sense of belonging and improves their social skills and self-awareness. They communicate their thoughts safely and avoid negative comments. They learn how to get along with others and express their ideas and emotions through different activities. In a warm, inclusive and safe atmosphere the children cherish this opportunity to communicate. In the Circle, teachers and students are on an equal footing which helps them understand each other, reduces isolation, promotes listening and appreciation of others.

In Circles, teachers are not only guides and listeners but participants and sharers. The traditional teacher-centred approach is replaced by an equal and trusting relationship, so teachers better understand their students and provide them with teaching content and methods that meet their needs and interests. Teachers also use weekly Circles to share their own experiences and get support and feedback from colleagues and managers.

Circle Solutions not only addresses students' social and emotional development, but also pays attention to teacher mental health. We have established a Wellbeing Centre in the school based on Circle Solutions principles where both Circle trainers and counsellors have helped to make the school more positive, inclusive, open-minded and innovative.

I have witnessed the huge changes Circle Solutions has brought to the school in the last three years. Our students are more confident, friendly and cooperative, our teachers more equal, trusting and professional and our managers more empowering, supportive and innovative. By creating a friendly and harmonious atmosphere Circle Solutions has improved the wellbeing of the whole school.

Lily.L.J.Lui, Principal, Dehong Chinese International School Xian

Building on what is working

Most schools are already using some or all of the ASPIRE principles in a myriad of different ways, often without fully realising this. It is valuable to appreciate what is already in place and working well so that staff and students can explore ways to develop this.

Educational psychologists are often positioned as professionals who carry out assessments with children and recommend interventions. But a unitary focus on this role limits their potential to support educational change. They invariably have substantial knowledge of school systems, child development, behaviour, relationships, motivation, learning and wellbeing as well as skills in observation, communication and collaborative practices. Many are more than happy to work with schools proactively to develop effective ways of enhancing learning and wellbeing for all. This is just one example.

Educational Psychologists supporting schools with ASPIRE in England

Educational Psychologists at Hampshire and Isle of Wight Educational Psychology Service have been using the strengths-based ASPIRE framework to support schools' wellbeing practice.

The Strengths in Circles Cards comprise 42 statements – 7 for each of the ASPIRE principles. These show what these principles mean in practice such as 'We are kind to each other' and 'We show gratitude'. The EPs shared these with Special Educational Needs Co-ordinators (SENCos) who then went together for a 'learning walk' around the school to look for evidence of each statement in practice. Notes were made and photos taken each time practice that illustrated one of the statements was identified. This was not just what was visible but also verbal interactions. As well as classrooms we went around the building, including the reception area.

SENCos found the framework easy to understand and enjoyed the learning walk observations and sharing photos with the whole staff team, generating discussion on good practice across the school. One SENCo planned to share Strengths in Circles cards with pupils who could blu-tac them to things they saw which showed how the statement was true. This has helped staff understand how to support relationships and wellbeing in a respectful and empowering way.

An audit tool was created using the "We ..." statements under each heading of the ASPIRE framework. It is planned that this tool will be used by schools (with their EP) to audit each area of the framework by considering whether each statement is enhanced, established, developing or not yet developing, listing examples of good practice and/or next steps depending on the level chosen. This audit tool has been shared with schools at a well-being conference run by Hampshire and IOW Educational Psychology and was well received.

Sam Cox and Anna Beasley, Educational Psychologists – Hampshire and Isle of Wight

Photographs taken by children are considered a valuable way to explore experiences in children's daily lives (Dockett et al., 2017).

Schools in context

Each person is both wonderfully unique and part of our shared humanity, having things in common with others. So are schools! There is no one-size-fits-all. People will have their own priorities, circumstances, needs and resources. This is illustrated by the initiative in South Africa building wellbeing across six schools with the ASPIRE principles guiding the process and supporting sustainability.

The Franschhoek Wellbeing Initiative in South Africa

There is a small town situated in a beautiful valley in South Africa, where six school communities, both primary and secondary, comprising 4000 children, their parents, teachers and other staff members pursue a shared vision to enhance the quality of life in the community. They are doing this through the implementation of a holistic wellbeing process. Each school has a wellbeing support team and a wellbeing coordinating committee functioning across the six schools, who have been overseeing the sustainability of the process for the past 7 years. The members of the committee are often asked "*How is this possible?*" The answer to this sustainability question is the ASPIRE framework applied as a critical lens for reflecting on the process.

The implementation of the holistic school wellbeing process, enhances Agency of pupils, staff and parents by providing access to opportunities where they can voice needs and challenges, share ideas to promote health and wellbeing, address challenges and learn to listen to one another. These opportunities involve small group discussion, WhatsApp group chats and feedback reports. During one of the discussion sessions conducted to get feedback on the process, a Grade 7 pupil to everyone's surprise confidently challenged the school principal about the discipline in the school, stating: "*Sir, if I may say, I do not agree with your viewpoint.*"

In the secondary schools, learners took the initiative in organizing their own wellbeing interventions. A student council member excellently explained the holistic wellbeing process to a group of stakeholders who visited the school. Teachers who initially questioned the process became advocates for the promotion of health and wellbeing. Unemployed parents started volunteering at the school with pride and confidence. In essence, members took agency for the promotion of health and wellbeing in their own contexts.

The physical and emotional Safety of learners are enhanced through interventions such as Kind Kids Month – during which kindness in various forms and across various levels of engagement have been enhanced. Just picture the ripple effect of 4000 learners each wearing a KIND KIDS bracelet, designing posters to enhance kindness in their specific contexts. Concurrently, discussing challenges associated with unsafe spaces, to ensure that pupils and staff are in touch with the impact of unkind acts and the importance of practicing kindness every day. Annual workshops to prepare primary school Grade 7 pupils to access secondary school provide opportunities to address their fears. Collaboration with a non-profit organization which provides individual psychosocial support enables teachers to make sure that pupils in distress have a safe space to go.

The deliberate enhancement of Positivity as a way to challenge the negative mindset that focus on problems rather than on assets and solutions gained ground as the process developed. A slow and sometimes lonely process for those who initially chose this road less travelled. Yet gradually more members noted the benefits of a positive take on life – pupils reporting that positive input from peers and teachers enhance their confidence; teachers acknowledged that they have a new and more grateful perspective on life; parents understanding why supporting their children is an investment in the future. In the process, challenges became opportunities to find solutions together and building a more hopeful future. A positive mindset clearly enhanced the relationships across all as the schools introduced teacher and parents appreciation days. Members across all levels started to appreciate one another's role in their school communities.

The appreciation and joy associated with being Included unconditionally, irrespective of role, status or academic achievement to participate in the holistic wellbeing process. Amazing stories of visiting places never seen before due to socio-economic challenges; broadened horizons through personal development workshops for secondary school learners, dress-up days for the primary school learners; facilitating participation in sport and cultural events in collaboration with non-profit organization for more pupils; inviting parents to be part of family funs days over weekend when they are available. The responses when pupils realise that there are no conditions for inclusion in this process, just a decision to participate, is priceless. Especially for those pupils and parents who have always been looking on from the margins. The connectedness resulting from these cross-level engagements contributes to a positive school climate.

The emphasis on Respectful engagements as a basis for the promotion of health and wellbeing enhanced the recognition of every individual as a worthy member of the school community. Teachers admitted how their struggle to accept some parents and pupils based on their circumstances turned into understanding and care as lived values. Each member is seen as important and recognised as contributing to the holistic wellbeing process. Values are no longer simply displayed as words, but lived through appreciative engagements, care and an willingness to see the other as a fellow human being on which my wellbeing depend, and whose wellbeing I impact – I am because you are.

The sound of Equity echoes through all the activities as the teams relentlessly work to keep as many members involved in the process, with the aim of enhancing the quality of life of each member to remove the barriers that might impact on their health and wellbeing. Each academic year starts with a motivational intervention – 'Future me' – to encourage all pupils to do their best. In this process power plays are challenged to ensure that the strength lies in the power of unity rather than power over others. Communication bridges are built across all levels of the system to open up ongoing conversations about moving closer to the shared vision. We are enhancing the quality of life in the community through the implementation of a holistic wellbeing process infused with the ASPIRE principles.

Prof Ansie Kitching, University of the Western Cape, South Africa

Sam and Anna identified different ways that schools were enacting ASPIRE, and Ansie has written about the myriad of actions supporting wellbeing and learning in what are often challenging circumstances. This is why the checklist below is not set in stone. What is likely to happen is that when people start paying serious (and playful!) attention to the context of wellbeing and learning in school, positive practice often snowballs.

ASPIRE checklist

	This is in place – we know it is effective because …	*This is the impact on various stakeholders*	*This is how we might extend our practice*	*Working on it – our actions to date are …*	*Just started – our next step will be …*
AGENCY					
SAFETY					
POSITIVITY					
INCLUSION					
RESPECT					
EQUITY					

And finally …

What do students say about being in school – do they feel empowered, safe, enjoy learning, feel they belong and are respected? Do they believe that people genuinely care about their learning and wellbeing, and are they able to access what is on offer, develop their strengths and make progress? Do they wake up on a Monday morning looking forward to being in school?

What do teachers say about working in school? Do they feel empowered, safe and respected? Do they enjoy being there and feel supported and nourished? Do they have opportunities to face challenges, with help if necessary, and grow in their understanding and practice? Do they anticipate kindness and trust? Do they wake up on a Monday morning looking forward to the week ahead?

What do families and communities say about the school? Do they feel confident that the school has their child's best interests at heart? Do they feel safe about coming and talking to teachers about their concerns, and are there opportunities to ask questions and for clarification? Is their culture and context recognised and taken account of?

I went to a conference recently, and one of the presenters – a recent graduate – talked about her experiences in education. She used a phrase which surprised me. She talked about the need for 'radical love'. But when I thought about it, I came to the conclusion that this is the essence of ASPIRE. Each principle looks fairly simple and is in fact commonplace, but when put into practice can be revolutionary. Not just a fleeting emotion or experience but a way of connecting the private and public sphere. What happens with individuals, in schools and in communities changes values, beliefs, relationships and priorities. This can, over time, change the world we live in now, the world our children will inherit and the world our students and schools construct together. It can build hope.

References and further reading

Dockett, S., Einarsdottir, J. & Perry, B. (2017). Photo elicitation: reflecting on multiple sites of meaning. *International Journal of Early Years Education, 25*(3), 225–240.

Jo, H., Ikei, H. & Miyazaki, Y. (2022). Physiological and psychological benefits of viewing an autumn foliage mountain landscape image among young women. *Forests, 13*(9), 1492.

Liu, Q., Wang, X., Liu, J., An, C., Liu, Y., Fan, X. & Hu, Y. (2021). Physiological and psychological effects of nature experiences in different forests on young people. *Forests, 12*(10), 1391.

McCree, M., Cutting, R. & Sherwin, D. (2020). The Hare and the Tortoise go to Forest School: taking the scenic route to academic attainment via emotional wellbeing outdoors. In J. Murray & I. Palaiologou (Eds.), *Young Children's Emotional Experiences* (106–122). Routledge.

Roffey, S. & Deal, R. (2015). *Strengths in Circles: Building Groups that Flourish and Fly*. Innovative Resources.

Other sources and further reading

Grenville-Cleave, B., Gudmundsdottir, D., Huppert, F., King, V., Roffey, D., Roffey, S. & De Vries, M. (2021). *Creating the World we Want to Live In: How Positive Psychology Can Build a Brighter Future*. Routledge.

Roffey, S. (2007). Transformation and emotional literacy: the role of school leaders in developing a caring community. *Leading and Managing, 13*(1), 16–30.

Sirkko, R., Kyrönlampi, T. & Puroila, A.M. (2019). Children's agency: opportunities and constraints. *International Journal of Early Childhood, 51*, 283–300.

Index

ability 9, 15–16, 19, 24, 31, 47, 53–54, 76, 87, 112–113, 116, 122, 131

absence 27, 60, 75, 108, 114

abuse 15–16, 19, 27–28, 33, 43, 74, 105, 109, 123

aboriginal 16, 74, 98, 108

acceptance 26

access 6, 58, 75, 107, 120–123, 127, 130, 139

active learning 10, 12, 14

adaptation 5, 10, 71, 76, 108, 117–118, 121–122

adversity 10–11, 48, 71

agents of change 13, 131

alienation 20, 71, 74, 83

Allen, K-A. 78

altruism 68, 72, 87–88

amygdala 35, 48

anger/angry 10, 20, 34, 37, 48, 50, 52, 56, 76, 98, 108, 123, 125

anxiety 12–13, 27, 31, 34, 36, 38, 43, 46, 48, 52, 55–56, 58, 64, 74, 76, 78, 84, 93, 117

assertiveness 10, 48

attendance 2, 27, 74–75, 86, 110

attention 27, 30–31, 50, 54–58, 64, 91, 94, 113, 115, 122, 134

australia 6, 14–15, 28, 30, 32, 36, 74, 118, 121, 131

behaviourist 19–20

belief 4–7, 9, 11, 15–16, 18–19, 45–47, 51, 73, 77, 80–81, 90–91, 95, 110–111, 120–123, 131, 139

belonging 5, 9, 20, 50, 56, 71–87, 131, 134, 139

Berry, R. 132–133

blame 11, 13, 19, 38, 47, 52, 75, 97, 111, 123

boys 26, 32, 71, 79, 115

British Psychological Society 101

Bronfenbrenner, U. 3–4

bully/bullying 2, 5, 19, 26–28, 35–36, 39, 41–42, 46, 60, 74–75, 79, 86, 93, 101, 121, 131

calming 20, 29, 34–35, 53, 64, 95

canada 15–16, 79

care/caring/carer 3, 10, 14, 17, 19, 26–29, 33, 35, 47, 51, 53, 60, 71, 73–74, 81, 92, 96–98, 101, 108–110, 114–115, 119, 124, 137

celebration 12, 32, 61, 63, 71, 78, 81, 84, 86, 91, 123, 133

citizens/citizenship 1, 5, 13, 24, 43, 100, 109–111, 116, 118, 122

challenges 1–2, 14, 19–20, 27, 31–32, 37, 45, 47, 49–50, 55, 72, 77–78, 96–97, 107, 115, 128, 131, 136–137, 139

change 4, 9–13, 20, 24, 36, 43, 56, 62, 81–82, 96–97, 101, 108–109, 114, 123, 131, 135, 139

checklists 23, 42, 67, 86, 104, 127, 138

child development 2, 5, 7, 10–11, 33, 37, 46, 92, 135

children's rights 3, 10, 27, 32–33, 45, 74, 92, 99–100, 104, 109, 120

china 6, 134

choice/choosing 3, 5, 9–14, 19–22, 29, 38, 49–50, 54, 58, 72, 91, 95, 114–115, 118, 120, 121, 124

Circle Solutions 20, 31, 38, 40, 62–65, 83, 94, 102, 124, 134

climate change 12–13, 18, 43

collaboration/collaborative 5, 15, 24, 31, 43, 46, 49–50, 58, 60, 72, 92, 108, 111–112, 115, 117, 127, 132, 135–137

cognition/cognitive 5, 27, 45, 48–50, 61, 76, 80, 91, 113, 132

communication 45, 51, 67, 73, 75, 80, 82, 91, 94, 98, 101, 104, 111, 119, 122, 135, 137 competence/competencies 2, 7, 9, 11–12, 30, 49–51, 73, 96, 112

competition 5, 31, 38, 79, 111–112, 120

compliance 19, 20, 51, 58, 74–76, 95, 97, 114

confidence 7, 11, 20, 24, 27–28, 31, 36–37, 49–51, 73, 92–93, 100, 116, 124–125, 134, 136, 139

conflict 6, 35, 38, 43, 50, 53, 56, 82, 95, 97, 108, 111, 114, 117, 124

consultation 20, 23, 98

context/contextual 3, 5, 9–10, 14–15, 18, 38, 55, 60–61, 71, 73, 78, 80, 83, 92, 108, 110, 113, 116, 122, 128, 135–137, 139

control 1, 5, 11–19, 23, 33–34, 37, 49, 52, 55–56, 75, 77, 79, 115, 123

conversations 4, 14, 30, 32, 35–37, 51, 56, 58, 61, 65, 67–68, 77, 83–84, 94–98, 113, 116, 119, 123, 131, 137

cooperation/cooperative 28, 31, 76, 98, 116–117, 134

courtesy 45–46, 93–95, 104, 118, 132

Covid-19 *see* pandemic

Cox, S. & Beasley A. 135

creativity 1–3, 7, 10, 15, 27, 47–50, 56, 59, 91, 123

critical thinking 3, 14–15, 72, 111–112, 115

criticism 46, 54, 92, 94

culture: community 5, 10–11, 15–16, 32, 45, 73, 75, 78, 81, 92–93, 98, 101, 108–109, 124, 137, 139; school/class 4–5, 16–17, 23, 28, 36, 38, 50, 54–61, 80, 82, 91, 93, 95, 100, 111, 118, 131

curious/curiosity 1, 7, 10, 14, 37, 49, 132

curriculum 1–2, 6, 10, 12, 16–19, 28, 42, 49, 60, 73, 79–80, 91–92, 98, 100, 107–108, 112, 120–123, 134

decision/decision-making 5, 9–21, 24, 27, 29, 38, 72, 92, 95, 98, 113, 132, 137

depression 12, 27, 36, 43, 48, 61, 101, 123

dignity 73, 90–92, 100, 109, 121

disadvantage 2–3, 27, 57, 60, 74, 107–112, 116–119, 122, 128

discipline 18, 26, 34, 92, 97, 110, 136

discrimination 1, 71, 74, 77, 91, 99, 107, 115, 124

digital safety 5, 26, 36, 42

disability 36, 40, 71, 75, 107–109, 121–122

Disabled Living Foundation 121

diversity 5–7, 30, 58, 71–72, 77–79, 86–87, 91–95, 100–101, 112, 120–121, 127–128, 131

DSM-5 101

Dutton, J.E. & Spreitzer, G.M. 95–96

Dweck, C. 47

early intervention 28, 110, 123

economic/economy 1, 4, 10, 43, 46, 71, 87, 107–111, 122, 128, 137

educational psychologists 7, 97, 135

efficacy 7, 9–11, 57, 131

emotions 19–20, 27, 29, 32, 34–35, 47–58, 72, 76, 82, 108, 116, 123, 134

emotional: competencies/intelligence/literacy/ skills 7, 28, 34, 49, 80, 91, 95, 97, 131; learning (SEL) 6, 21, 38, 63, 83, 102, 124, 132, 134; needs 7, 97; regulation 19, 29, 32, 53, 101, 115–116; resources 98; safety 5, 26, 29, 33, 43, 97, 136; support 27, 73, 114–115; wellbeing 2, 33, 45, 58, 71, 132

empathy 13, 26, 28, 36, 52, 62, 65, 68, 71–72, 75, 77–82, 80, 95, 97, 110, 116

empowering 12–13, 18, 75, 95, 100, 116, 134–135, 139, 24

engagement 1, 3, 5, 7, 11–20, 28, 50, 53–60, 71, 74, 78–81, 94, 101, 111, 118–120, 131–137

environment 6, 18, 22, 57, 92, 132; learning/ school 1–2, 6, 14, 17, 26, 28–33, 37–38, 49, 58, 71, 73–74, 77–78, 91, 96–97, 105, 108, 110, 118, 120–123, 132; social 9–10, 35, 46, 50, 75, 92, 107, 113, 115, 123

Estonia 3, 112

exclusion 27, 36, 71, 74, 76–77, 79, 82, 101, 112, 117, 121

exclusive belonging 72

expectations 10, 13, 18–19, 30, 46–47, 52, 60–61, 68, 75, 77, 80, 96–97, 101, 107–108, 122, 124

experiences 1, 7, 13–15, 27, 30, 45–46, 76, 95–96, 101, 114, 121, 123, 132, 134–135, 139

ethics 48, 91

facilitation 10–11, 14, 18, 55, 81–82, 94, 96, 102, 111, 120, 123, 137

failure 31, 51, 111

fairness 1, 6, 53, 73, 77–78, 91, 107, 110–116, 118, 120, 124, 127

family 1–7, 10–11, 16, 26–28, 37, 40, 43, 46–47, 52–53, 62, 71–82, 84, 87, 90–91, 96–99, 101, 107–110, 113–114, 117–124, 131–132, 137, 139

Farr, T. 96

fear 20, 26–27, 30, 33–34, 36, 48, 51, 75–76, 82, 108, 136

Finland 3, 60, 91, 112
flexibility 6, 14, 49, 55, 75, 86, 95, 107, 116–117, 120–121, 127–128
friends/friendly/friendship 10, 27, 32, 36–39, 42, 51, 54, 57–58, 60, 63, 65, 71, 73, 76, 79, 83, 86, 95, 113, 116, 134
Fullan, M. 80
fun 45, 48–50, 53–54, 56, 59, 63, 117–118
future 1, 5–7, 10, 13, 17, 18, 24, 32, 37, 43, 58, 61, 68, 71, 87, 105, 108–112, 114, 116, 122, 128, 133, 136–137

gender 32, 56, 71, 79, 91, 107, 115, 124
Glasser, W. 19
goals/goal-setting 1, 12, 17, 47, 72–73, 79, 92, 96, 109, 120
Goodenow, C. & Grady, K.E. 73
gratitude 5, 46, 61, 65, 67–68, 135–136
Gray, P. 49

happiness 2, 11–12, 38, 43, 46, 72, 78, 112, 126
Hansberry, B. 82
Hart, R. 17
Hattie, J. 94
Hoyle, T. 59
human rights 3, 6, 16, 22, 92, 121
Hussein, F. 100
hypotheticals 21–22, 38, 40, 84, 103

inequality 1–2, 108–112, 120, 124
imagination 12, 14, 22, 49–52, 59, 64–65, 91, 123
inclusive belonging 72
independent/independence 3, 7, 9–11, 14, 49, 109, 114, 121
indigenous 15–16, 74, 98, 107
integrity 92, 96
interaction/interactive 3–7, 10, 12–13, 15, 24, 29, 34, 46–47, 49–51, 77–80, 91, 93, 96, 98, 104, 113, 116, 126, 132, 135
interest(s) 12–15, 22–23, 27–29, 32, 46, 49, 51–52, 54, 62, 71–73, 76, 79, 83–84, 92, 94, 97–100, 111, 115, 119, 128, 134, 139

judgment 5, 12–13, 37, 50, 72, 75, 85, 91–92, 96, 101, 108, 119

kindness 1, 5, 26, 30, 36, 39, 42–43, 45–46, 50, 54, 56–58, 62, 67–68, 72, 77, 84, 90, 93–94, 101, 118, 135–136, 139
Kitching, A. 136–137

labels/labelling 26, 75, 80, 93, 101, 115
language 5, 7, 12, 14–16, 31, 45, 47, 51, 53, 55, 74, 81, 86, 91, 93–95, 98, 100–101, 107–108, 113, 115–116, 118, 125
laughter/laughing 31, 50–51, 54, 56, 61, 63, 66, 125
leaders/leadership 3–4, 7, 13, 20–21, 28, 37, 47, 58, 60–61, 80, 92, 95–96, 100, 111, 120, 124, 131
learning environment *see* environment
listening 5, 10, 14, 19, 22, 28, 30, 37, 46, 52, 54, 58, 62, 64, 73, 84, 92–96, 98–99, 102, 104, 116, 118, 122, 134, 136
literacy 7, 113–114, 116, 118–119; for emotional literacy *see* emotional
Liu, L. 134
loss 108, 123
love 26, 46, 51, 56, 59, 73, 77, 96, 109, 113, 115, 123, 132, 139; of learning 1, 3
LSE 110

Mandela, N. 111
Martela, F. 11
mattering 73
McNally, S. 97
meaning 1–2, 11–13, 16, 33, 45, 47, 58, 61, 73, 101, 123
meetings 21, 37, 61–62, 98–99, 104, 113, 119, 121
mental health 1–7, 27, 32–33, 43, 46, 49, 60, 72–76, 100, 107–108, 110, 116, 134
Miezis, J. 131–132
mindfulness 64
mindset 45, 47, 51, 65, 114, 136
mistakes 5, 11, 20, 27, 31, 39, 42, 55–56, 65, 92, 125
Montessori, M. 49
motivation 2, 5, 7, 10–15, 19, 24, 31, 51–52, 55, 58, 60, 74, 78, 81, 97–98, 101, 111, 135, 137

NAPCAN 32–33
nature/natural 6, 14, 49, 68, 114, 122–123, 132–133
negative: effects/experiences 7, 19, 27, 35–36, 46, 49–50, 75–76, 95, 107, 111; emotions/feelings 5, 47–48, 51, 54, 56, 76; labels 26; self-concept 52–53; talk/interactions/thinking 45–46, 57–58, 65, 68, 77, 92, 94, 98, 134, 136
NSW Commission for Children & Young People 53

Obama, B. 90
O'Brien M. & Blue, L. 55
OECD 12, 91, 112, 120
online 2, 26, 36, 49, 71–72
oracy 7, 116
optimism 5, 11, 46, 48, 51, 61
ownership 10, 12, 17, 28
outcomes 1, 3, 7, 9–11, 14, 19, 27, 36, 45, 54, 56, 58, 60–61, 82, 95–98, 108, 110–112, 116, 119
outside spaces 29, 58, 65, 122

Paley, V. 77
pandemic 2, 9, 17, 19, 28, 43, 46, 74, 107, 111, 113, 134
parents/carers 4, 10–11, 14, 17, 27, 29, 33–34, 36–37, 46–53, 59, 62–63, 71, 73–76, 80–83, 92–94, 97–98, 101, 107–124, 136–137
participation 5, 9, 17–19, 51, 54, 71, 82, 92, 98, 117, 121, 124, 136–137
passive/passivity 10, 15, 50
pedagogy 5, 12, 55, 80, 98, 134
peers 2–3, 7, 26, 36, 46, 53, 59–60, 72–74, 77–79, 82, 100, 117, 120–123, 136
personal best 5, 31, 79
physical health 1, 27, 33–35, 47, 49, 58, 75–76, 91–92, 108, 110–113, 119, 122, 128, 134
Pink, D. 12
play 5, 7, 13–14, 27, 34, 45, 48–50, 52–54, 58–60, 67, 76–77, 79, 81, 83, 110, 112–115, 122, 132
playfulness 5, 50, 56, 58, 67, 96, 137
playground 11, 17, 29, 40, 49, 58–61, 113, 125–126
policies 4, 18, 20–21, 23, 26, 28–29, 33, 36–38, 42, 47, 58, 62, 71, 75, 82–83, 96, 98, 100, 104, 107, 111–112, 116, 120–121, 124, 127
poverty 43, 46, 75, 80, 107, 109, 111
Power, Threat, Meaning Framework 101
pride/proud 11, 32, 45, 48, 56, 79, 83, 92, 117, 132, 136
Prilleltensky, I. 73
problem solving 24, 27, 47–50, 53, 57–58, 112
progress 2, 4–5, 7, 23, 31, 49, 51, 73–78, 94, 112, 117, 120, 139
project(s) 6, 11, 15–17, 20, 22, 55, 73, 79, 95, 117, 120, 132–133
Putnam, R.D. 72

Quinlan, D. 60

reflection 21, 57, 96, 134
relatedness 9, 11
relaxation 45, 60, 64, 132
religion 16, 71–72, 74, 90–92, 101, 107, 124
resilience 2–5, 7, 14, 17–18, 47–50, 60, 65, 71, 74, 76, 111, 132
responsibility 5, 9–12, 15, 19, 22, 24, 28–29, 32, 36, 38, 76, 82, 91, 97–99, 111, 116, 118, 122, 124
Restorative Justice/Practice 82, 86, 100
Rights Respecting Schools 99–100, 104
risk 19, 27, 29–31, 36–38, 43, 55, 82, 94, 119
role models 22, 26–27, 32, 60, 115
Roots of Empathy 79–80
RSA 17
Rumble, T. 121–122
Ryan, R. & Deci, E. 9, 11

Sanna, F. 17
school climate 60, 80, 137
Scot 95
self: awareness/concept/esteem/sense of self 2–3, 7, 11, 16, 26, 31, 36, 43, 45–48, 51–53, 72, 76, 79–80, 92–95, 109, 115, 134; self-control/regulation 19, 49, 55, 132; self-determination 5, 9, 11–12; self-directed learning 5, 12, 15, 23; self-efficacy/reliance 9–10, 50, 57; self-protection 32, 34; self-respect 92–93, 95, 104, 109
Seligman, M. 47, 61
share/sharing 17–18, 21, 28, 45, 52–53, 55, 58, 60, 62, 72–73, 75, 77–78, 81, 93, 100, 111, 114, 116, 118, 124, 133–137
smile/smiling 53–54, 71, 78, 91–93, 125
social action 5, 13, 16–17, 23
solution focus 6, 37, 45, 47, 51, 63, 67, 81, 99, 134, 136
SOS Children's villages 53–54
South Africa 6, 135–137
Square Pegs 75
staff/staffroom 4, 6, 17, 20–21, 26, 30, 33–35, 37, 42, 46, 52, 58–63, 78, 80–81, 87, 95–97, 99, 101, 104, 108, 112, 116, 119, 124, 127, 131–136
stories 5, 12, 14, 32, 52, 65, 77–78, 81, 96, 102, 114, 137
strengths 5, 7, 12–13, 29–30, 45–48, 51, 57–64, 67, 79, 115, 117, 132, 134–135, 139

Strengths in Circles cards 21, 39, 63, 84, 102, 124, 135
Sure Start 110, 113
system(s)/systemic 2–4, 6–7, 12, 37, 56, 60, 75, 90–91, 96–97, 108–112, 116, 120, 124, 128, 135, 137

teacher-student relationships 18–19, 30–31, 54, 61, 77–78, 94–95, 97
teacher wellbeing 3, 54, 60, 67, 97
tests/testing 12–13, 19, 58, 65, 79, 91, 112, 124
thankfulness 61, 65
Tidmund, L. 56, 58
Times Education Commission 110
touch 5, 33–35, 42, 113
trauma 35, 42–43, 49, 96–97, 101, 108–109, 123–124
trust 17, 19, 26–27, 29–30, 34, 36–37, 39–40, 46, 50, 58, 62, 73, 91–96, 102, 104, 111–112, 124, 128, 134, 139
toys 14, 29, 35, 56, 79, 85, 97, 99, 114–115

UCL/IoE/NTU 80
UNCROC *see* children's rights
understanding 1, 5, 7, 10–16, 24, 27–28, 30, 33, 37, 50, 72–79, 82–83, 92, 94, 97, 99–100, 112–113, 116, 118, 120, 136–137, 139
uniform 83

values 1, 10, 12, 21–22, 45, 56, 60, 68, 72, 77, 83, 92, 100–101, 108, 111–112, 118–119, 131, 134, 137, 139
Van Deur, P.A. & Murray-Harvey, R. 15
vision 7, 21, 47, 60, 95, 131, 136–137
vulnerability 2, 27, 29, 46, 74, 80, 105, 124

welcoming 2, 54, 72, 77–78, 81, 84, 86, 94, 97, 100, 118
Wellbeing Stories 65
whole school 17, 36, 45, 60, 62, 80, 100, 132, 134
Wilkinson, R. 128
Wingspread Declaration on School Connections 73